DEMCO

Rihanna

by Laurie J. Edwards

LUCENT BOOKS
A part of Gale, Cengage Learning

GALE
CENGAGE Learning™

Detroit • New York • San Francisco • New Haven, Conn • Waterville, Maine • London

LIBRARY OF CONGRESS CATALOGING-IN-PUBLICATION DATA

Edwards, Laurie J.
  Rihanna / by Laurie J. Edwards.
    p. cm. — (People in the news)
  Includes bibliographical references and index.
  ISBN 978-1-4205-0129-2 (hardcover)
  1. Rihanna, 1988—Juvenile literature. 2. Singers—Biography—Juvenile literature. I. Title.
  ML3930.R44E39 2009
  782.42164092—dc22
  [B]
                                        2008051290

Lucent Books
27500 Drake Rd.
Farmington Hills, MI 48331

ISBN-13: 978-1-4205-0129-2
ISBN-10: 1-4205-0129-1

Dedication: To my family and favorite "critters" for their ongoing encouragement and support.

Contents

Fame and celebrity are alluring. People are drawn to those who walk in fame's spotlight, whether they are known for great accomplishments or for notorious deeds. The lives of the famous pique public interest and attract attention, perhaps because their experiences seem in some ways so different from, yet in other ways so similar to, our own.

Newspapers, magazines, and television regularly capitalize on this fascination with celebrity by running profiles of famous people. For example, television programs such as *Entertainment Tonight* devote all of their programming to stories about entertainment and entertainers. Magazines such as *People* fill their pages with stories of the private lives of famous people. Even newspapers, newsmagazines, and television news frequently delve into the lives of well-known personalities. Despite the number of articles and programs, few provide more than a superficial glimpse at their subjects.

Lucent's People in the News series offers young readers a deeper look into the lives of today's newsmakers, the influences that have shaped them, and the impact they have had in their fields of endeavor and on other people's lives. The subjects of the series hail from many disciplines and walks of life. They include authors, musicians, athletes, political leaders, entertainers, entrepreneurs, and others who have made a mark on modern life and who, in many cases, will continue to do so for years to come.

These biographies are more than factual chronicles. Each book emphasizes the contributions, accomplishments, or deeds that have brought fame or notoriety to the individual and shows how that person has influenced modern life. Authors portray their subjects in a realistic, unsentimental light. For example, Bill Gates—the cofounder and chief executive officer of the software giant Microsoft—has been instrumental in making personal computers the most vital tool of the modern age. Few dispute his business savvy, his perseverance, or his technical expertise, yet critics say he is ruthless in his dealings with competitors and driven more by his desire to maintain Microsoft's dominance in the computer industry than by an interest in furthering technology.

In these books, young readers will encounter inspiring stories about real people who achieved success despite enormous obstacles. Oprah Winfrey—the most powerful, most watched, and wealthiest woman on television today—spent the first six years of her life in the care of her grandparents while her unwed mother sought work and a better life elsewhere. Her adolescence was colored by promiscuity, pregnancy at age fourteen, rape, and sexual abuse.

Each author documents and supports his or her work with an array of primary and secondary source quotations taken from diaries, letters, speeches, and interviews. All quotes are footnoted to show readers exactly how and where biographers derive their information and provide guidance for further research. The quotations enliven the text by giving readers eyewitness views of the life and accomplishments of each person covered in the People in the News series.

In addition, each book in the series includes photographs, annotated bibliographies, timelines, and comprehensive indexes. For both the casual reader and the student researcher, the People in the News series offers insight into the lives of today's newsmakers—people who shape the way we live, work, and play in the modern age.

Barbados Cinderella

On an island in the sun, a baby entered the world one February day in 1988. Her parents named her Robyn Rihanna Fenty. No one knew then that this newborn would someday become a star. Nor did they realize her sunny island home of Barbados would provide the idea for her first album. But the baby born that February 20 had a date with destiny. A decade and a half later she took the stage name Rihanna, stunned the music world at age sixteen, and became part of a real, live fairy tale.

Once Upon a Time

Rihanna's Cinderella story began on Barbados, a Caribbean island with a warm climate and friendly people. A bit smaller than New York City, Barbados is home to about 300,000 people, unlike New York, which teems with a population of more than 8 million. Islanders are called Barbadians or, more popularly, Bajans. Bajan is also the name of the language, a mixture of British and West African, sometimes called Barbadian Creole.

Proud to be a Bajan, Rihanna has honored her island not only by calling her first album *Music of the Sun* but also by using a trident as a backdrop for many of her appearances and album covers. The trident is a three-pronged spear for fishing that appears on the flag of Barbados. In turn, the island honored Rihanna. At the first Barbados Music Awards in 2006, she received eight awards. In February 2008 the minister of culture named her "Cultural Ambassador of Barbados."

The island of Barbados is more than Rihanna's birthplace; it is her heritage and her people. It is where she first learned to sing. She absorbed the island rhythms as she was growing up, and its

Although grateful for her successful singing career, Rihanna has learned that the cost of fame often includes the loss of privacy.

beat comes through in her music. She blended the Caribbean influences of soca and reggae music with hip-hop and rhythm and blues to create her own unique sound. This unusual fusion caught the attention of music producers and fans alike. In the summer of 2005 her first release, "Pon de Replay," showcased reggae "riddims"—Carribean instrumental rhythms—to create a catchy beat that made it a dance hall hit and started her on the road to stardom.

A Dream Come True

Rihanna's meteoric rise to fame may seem to be magic, but the truth is that Rihanna believed in herself and her dreams. Even more importantly, she worked hard to achieve them. To reach her dreams, she left behind her beloved island, her family, and her friends and moved to another country. She adjusted to a fast-paced life in New York. She worked long hours to produce her albums, perform on tours, and improve her craft. At times, when loneliness and exhaustion tarnished the glitter of stardom, she persevered. She gave it her all as she sang through the pain, much as she had as a young child who sang through the many heartaches of growing up.

Her strong work ethic and drive for success paid off. By 2008 twenty-year-old Rihanna had produced four albums that, between them, had spawned eleven Top 40 hit singles in the United States. All of her albums and many of her songs had gone platinum; some, multiplatinum. She had won countless awards, including a Grammy. Rihanna had achieved her childhood dream: to make music all over the world.

She did not plan to stop with these achievements, however. As she told interviewer Chris Rolls of MP3.com, "I try not to get comfortable at all, because I don't want to be satisfied at any success that I get. To me it's all working harder and trying to strive to get to the next level."[1] Motivated by a philosophy like this, Rihanna's journey has only just begun.

Chapter 1

Her Island Home

Young Rihanna, holding a broomstick as a microphone stand, imitated her idol, Mariah Carey. With a hairbrush for a microphone, she performed in front of her mirror. The neighbors complained about how loudly she sang, but Rihanna did not let that stop her. Instead, she sang her way through the headaches and heartaches of her childhood. "All I wanted to do was to make music all over the world,"[2] Rihanna says.

Like many young teens in the 1990s, she grew up listening to and imitating Mariah Carey. Unlike Carey, she did not live near New York City. Instead, her home was Barbados, a small Caribbean island far from the bustling music world of New York— not the best place for an aspiring music star to be discovered.

A Perfect Setting

From the air, Barbados appears to be a tiny pearl in a necklace of islands stretching from the tip of Florida to northeastern Venezuela. Bounded by the Caribbean on the west and the Atlantic Ocean on the east, this small island—with its tropical breezes, abundant white beaches, and crystal-clear water—is often called a Caribbean paradise.

Life on the island was not all idyllic, however. The young couple who were to become Rihanna's parents met during high school. Although they loved each other, Monica and Ronald Fenty fought frequently. Ronald had endured a rough childhood; he

Rihanna comes from the Caribbean island of Barbados, which is known for its white beaches, blue sky, and tropical breezes.

started scoring marijuana and crack cocaine on the streets at age fourteen. Many of their fights centered around his drug habits. In spite of their differences, they married in 1985.

Ronald and Monica established a home and within two years began to prepare for the birth of their first child. Little did they know what life had in store for their daughter. They were young and likely unprepared for the stresses a baby would bring to their already troubled marriage.

A Star Is Born

Robyn Rihanna Fenty was born on February 20, 1988. Her parents chose a first name that began with the letter *R*, as they would for both her brothers. *Robyn* is an alternate spelling for *Robin*, meaning "bright fame." It is also the name of

An Early Memory

Although young Rihanna was a tomboy, she later came to love dressing up and putting on makeup. Today her fans admire her numerous tattoos and signature fingernail designs. Asked by a reporter about her first memory related to her fingernails, Rihanna says:

> I was 4, and my great-grandma was watching us. I used to give her so much trouble. She probably yelled at me, so I went into my mom's room, took her nail polishes, opened them, and painted "bracelets" up my arm. Then I poured them into a toy hard hat my brother had. When my mom came home, she got really upset. I got scared because I thought, 'My gosh, I have to go to school like this! Because we never used to have nail polish remover.'

Quoted in Robin Sayers, "Beauty Talk with Rihanna," MSN Lifestyle, May 2008. http://lifestyle.msn.com/beautyandfashion/celebritystyle/articleinstyle.aspx?cp-documentid=6165495.

a red-breasted songbird. Both meanings fit the future star perfectly.

Her middle name, *Rihanna*, the name she later took as her stage name, has its roots in the Welsh name *Rhiannon*, meaning "great queen or goddess." *Rhiannon* was also the name of a princess in Welsh legends. Rihanna, too, was destined to become a princess in her own fairy tale. Her rise to fame distinguished her as the Barbados Cinderella.

The Headaches Begin

Like Cinderella, Rihanna had her share of childhood problems. She did not have two stepsisters, but instead had two younger brothers. Rorrey came along about two years after Rihanna was born. Rajad followed years later. Between the births of her two brothers, Rihanna began elementary school at Charles F. Broome Memorial School.

Around age eight, Rihanna began having excruciating headaches. The pain became so severe that her parents took her to a doctor. Though tests showed nothing physically wrong, the headaches continued for years. It was not until her parents separated when she was a young teen that the headaches finally disappeared. At that point, she realized they had come from hiding her emotions. Rihanna explains, "I wouldn't cry. I wouldn't get upset. It was just all in here [her head]. I had to go through a lot of CAT scans. They even thought it was a tumour, because it was that intense. It's not great memories. But it helped to build me and make me stronger."[3]

A Terrible Secret

Rihanna's childhood was marred by more than her parents' quarrels. When she was young, her father sometimes left tinfoil in ashtrays around the house, but she did not understand what it meant. "I just knew that my mum didn't like it, and they were always fighting about it. My mother was a very strong woman and tried to shelter us from as much as she could. But she was working, and he was at home, so there was only so much that she could hide from us."[4]

During those years her mother worked hard to support the family. Sometimes her father stayed home to care for the children. Other times, he disappeared for days on end. Rihanna had no idea why until the day she peeked at her dad through a gap in the kitchen door and discovered his secret: He had been using the foil to smoke crack cocaine.

Her father recalls that day with clarity: "I turned and looked Rihanna in the eye and instantly came back down from the high I was on. I saw her run for her mother, ask her something and then they both started to cry. I had no idea she had been watching."[5]

Years later, after Rihanna rose to stardom, her father confessed his guilty secret to the newspapers:

> I will never forgive myself for what I did to her. I will always have nightmares as I think of her crying, begging me to stop. But I was a hopeless addict and I couldn't care. My beautiful daughter should never have witnessed the things she did.[6]

His addiction was hard on everyone, not only Rihanna. Reporter Suzannah Ramsdale describes this time in the family's life in the British magazine *Now*:

> Rihanna and her brothers, Rorrey and Rajad, watched helplessly as their father, Ronald Fenty, spiralled into addiction. . . . At his lowest he was reduced to scoring drugs on street corners and leaving drug paraphernalia around the house. . . . It got so bad they barely had enough money to eat as Ronald . . . desperately sought out his next fix. During this time, the singer took care of her brothers while mum Monica —now divorced from her dad—worked round-the-clock in accountancy to keep [support] the family.[7]

Absentee Mother

Her mother's long hours at work meant she was gone from home a lot. Monica Fenty needed to support her children, but she had another reason for being away so much. "My mom is very ambitious,"[8] Rihanna said years later when asked to explain her own drive to succeed.

Rihanna posing with her younger brother in 2007. Rihanna was a second mom to her two brothers because her mother was so busy with work.

While Monica's hard work was admirable, there was a darker side to why she was always busy. In describing her mother, Rihanna says, "She was a workaholic. If she took a week off from work, she got so miserable at home. She was like, 'Robyn, I have to do something. I have to do something.' She would just go to my aunt's store to help her work, just because she couldn't sit still."[9]

With neither of her parents around, tending to the boys often fell to Rihanna, who had to grow up quickly and take over the job of mothering her brothers. Too young to be handling all that responsibility, Rihanna recalls getting into conflicts with her brothers. She says, "We used to fight and when I say fight, I don't mean arguments, I mean physically fight. I hit the older one in his face with a glass bottle. My mom was pretty upset."[10]

Turnaround

Luckily for Rihanna and her brothers, their father regretted the pain he had caused his family. He realized his children were more important to him than drugs. Being kicked out of the house and out of their lives when Rihanna was nine led him to reevaluate his life. He says, "It was the turning point. Monica chucked me out and we never patched things up. I knew I could [continue] carrying on taking drugs and die or stop and see my children grow up. I still thank God every day I chose to stop—I live for my children now."[11] Although her parents later divorced, Rihanna now had a father she could count on.

Rihanna readily admits that her childhood was not easy, but she does not dwell on it. Instead, she prefers to focus on the good memories:

> It's fair to say I had a few humps and bumps along the way while growing up. But I think every child growing up goes through some sort of upheaval and perhaps mine was a bit worse. At the end of the day, I don't think about it any more and it doesn't make me angry. Despite Dad's problems, I still vividly remember all the good things like playing with him on the beach and catching crabs together.[12]

In addition to him playing with her and her brothers, Rihanna remembers the lessons her father taught her. "He taught me how to swim, fish, and ride; he's the one who made me tough and prepared me for the world."[13]

The Songbird

Although Rihanna's life left her with little reason to sing, her musical talent was obvious from a young age. She was only three when she first began to imitate her favorite singers. Nick Owens of the *Sunday Mirror* writes about her early love for music:

As a little girl, Rihanna bothered her neighbors with her loud singing. No one complains about her singing now.

Yet amid the chaos Rihanna, nicknamed Pinky, as she was called then, because she loved pink clothes, was blossoming into a singer. Aged three she would stand in front of the mirror, hairbrush in hand, singing along to Whitney Houston's "Saving All My Love For You." At seven she was displaying the incredible voice which today sells millions of records.[14]

Rihanna's father remembers hearing her croon "A Whole New World" from Disney's *Aladdin* when she was seven: "I was in the lounge and heard this angelic singing from the balcony. I looked out and it was Rihanna. My heart jumped. I knew then she was special."[15]

Not everyone appreciated her belting out songs from the balcony. The neighbors often complained about how loudly she sang, but Rihanna ignored them. Her grandmother Carla insisted it was in her blood and encouraged her to keep singing.

Rihanna may have been confident enough to warble songs at home, but shyness held her back from performing in public. To ease her stage fright, she formed a group with two friends. She sang lead; they sang backup. Their first success came at a school talent show in 2004. They won with their rendition of Mariah Carey's "Hero."

From Tomboy to Beauty Queen

Before she won the talent show, Rihanna had been a tomboy. Although she loved pink, she was not a girlie girl. Growing up, she preferred to dress in her brother's baggy pants and sneakers. She also drilled with the Barbados Cadet Corps (BCC). This military training organization for students, originally open only to boys, had begun accepting girls in the mid-1970s. Accepted into the BCC at age twelve, Rihanna proved she was tough by reaching the rank of corporal.

A dare from her classmates, though, sparked Rihanna's transformation from tomboy to Miss Combermere Beauty Pageant contestant in 2004. In the past she had laughed at pageants and called them stupid. Now she agreed to try. Her move into the limelight and her subsequent interest in clothes

The Barbados Cadet Corps

The Barbados Cadet Corps (BCC) began in 1904 and is one of the oldest youth organizations on the island. Students participate in military, school, and community activities to build self-esteem and learn discipline and respect. The BCC is part of the Barbados Defence Force, so the cadets train and drill like the military, but they mainly participate in ceremonial parades and do community service.

The BCC had this to say about Rihanna, or as she was known, Corporal Fenty:

> From very early in her international career, it was clear that she reflected many of the characteristics emphasized in the Barbados Cadet Corps and that she exuded a quiet self-confidence that we routinely see in our NCOs [noncommissioned officers]. . . .

> The BCC is extremely proud of the growth and success achieved by Rihanna over the past few years and of the dignity and poise with which she has handled the whole adventure . . . and we are proud of the role that the Cadet Corps has been able to play in molding assets like her. . . .

> Congratulations . . . and may you continue to live your school song, where "truest flame lies in high Endeavour." Keep the flame burning brightly.

Barbados Cadet Corps, "Congrats to Cultural Ambassador Rihanna." www.cadetcorps. bb/index.htm.

and makeup was a change for her, but Rihanna jokes, "My military training came in handy for learning to balance books on my head for the catwalk."[16] She also credits the Barbados Cadet Corps with helping her gain poise and confidence. That, along with her singing voice, helped her win the title and crown.

Rihanna's Big Break

A few months before her sixteenth birthday, Rihanna had an even greater thrill than winning a talent show or beauty contest. American music producer Evan Rogers was vacationing in the Caribbean with his Bajan-born wife, Jackie. Because Barbados had once been her home, Jackie had friends and family on the island. One of Rihanna's friends, who knew Jackie, introduced Rihanna to the couple, and Rogers agreed to listen to her sing.

Deep in her heart, Rihanna had always believed she would find a way to make her dreams come true. If she could show the world how talented she was, she felt certain success was in her future. She maintains, "I always knew I was gonna do this.

Mariah Carey

Rihanna makes no secret of her admiration for other singers. In addition to liking Alicia Keys and Beyoncé, she idolizes Mariah Carey. Interestingly enough, Rihanna's life has paralleled Carey's in several ways.

Mariah Carey, from Huntington, New York, also has parents who divorced when she was a child, and she faced childhood pain. Hers came in the form of racial prejudice, when neighbors allegedly set fire to her family's car and poisoned their dog. She, too, was discovered as a teenager and went on to become a star.

Carey began as a songwriter and backup singer for Brenda K. Starr. In 1988 Tommy Mottola, the president of Sony's music division, offered Carey a recording contract. Her first five singles hit number one and put her on the track to fame. Critics panned some of her midcareer efforts, but she made a comeback. In April 2008 she became second only to the Beatles in number of hit singles, when "Touch My Body" became her eighteenth song to hit number one.

Known for her wide vocal range, Carey has won five Grammys for her pop and rhythm-and-blues music. Her rise to fame, like Rihanna's, is often called a Cinderella story.

Many aspiring singers dream of being "discovered" as Kelly Clarkson, pictured, was on the American Idol TV show. But few have the talent or luck to make it happen like Rihanna did.

I would say, 'When I become a singer. . . .' I knew I was gonna meet somebody one day. Really and truly."[17]

And meet somebody she did. Evan Rogers had been instrumental in the making of the careers of many music stars, including Christina Aguilera and Kelly Clarkson. But could a shy fifteen-year-old put on a performance that would impress a big New York producer?

Chapter 2

A Bold
Move

As Rihanna and her friends stood poised to sing for Evan Rogers that day, all eyes were on them. The music executive seated before them would decide their fate. Getting an audition with a major New York music producer was Rihanna's first step on the road to stardom. She had only a short time to prove that she was good enough for the big time.

A Date with Destiny

Although she was nervous, Rihanna had determined to make the most of her opportunity. For the occasion, she dressed in pink capris, a pink shirt, and pink sneakers. She fought her nervousness and sang the song that won her the talent show, Mariah Carey's "Hero." She followed up with "Emotion" by Destiny's Child. As they had in the talent show, her two school friends sang backup. But for Rogers, Rihanna's performance stood out:

> The minute Rihanna walked into the room, it was like the other two girls didn't exist. She carried herself like a star even when she was 15. But the killer was when she opened her mouth to sing. She was a little rough around the edges, but she had this edge to her voice.[18]

Rogers was interested enough to ask for another audition—this time with Rihanna alone.

Evan Rogers and Carl Sturken

Since the 1980s, Evan Rogers and Carl Sturken's songs have propelled many stars up the charts. In 1991 they sang with their own group, Rhythm Syndicate. Their pop song "P.A.S.S.I.O.N." became a number-one hit. After two years of touring, they became full-time songwriters and music producers.

In 1998 their song "(God Must Have Spent) A Little More Time on You," sung by 'N Sync, moved to number eight on the charts, and "All That I Need," performed by Boyzone, went to number one. In the early 2000s their songs helped launch pop singers Christina Aguilera, Mandy Moore, and Jessica Simpson to the top of the charts.

In 2005 they formed Syndicated Rhythm Productions and marketed Rihanna. They went on to sign others, including Shontelle, J-Status, the Urgency, and Javier. Later they collaborated on a publishing deal with Universal Music and worked with Anastacia, Mikaila, and Innosense.

A Grammy-nominated team, by 2008 they had more than twenty top-forty hits, twelve top-five hits, and six BMI (Broadcast Music, Inc.) Awards. Their songs are found on more than 60 million albums sold around the world.

A Golden Opportunity

Rihanna's impromptu concert with her friends in Rogers's hotel room had moved her one step closer to her dream, but now that the producer had singled her out for a second audition, she needed to prove she had the star quality he was seeking. Her mother accompanied her to the audition, and Rihanna, who had no time to change, was still dressed in her school uniform.

She may have looked more like a schoolgirl than star material, but her voice captured Rogers's attention. When she finished this second performance, he invited her to come to the United States to meet his partner, Carl Sturken, and record a demo tape.

Bright Lights, Big City

In the Cinderella story, a fairy godmother whisks Cinderella to the ball in a pumpkin carriage. In Rihanna's fairy tale, her fairy godfather flew her to New York City in a plane to record her singing. Throughout the next year Rihanna and her mother traveled back and forth from Barbados so she could make the tape. Once she turned sixteen, with her mother's permission, Rihanna left school in Barbados and moved to the United States to live with Rogers and his wife in Stamford, Connecticut.

Going from a small island to Manhattan Island, where New York City is located, could have been overwhelming. New York City is only slightly larger than Barbados, but it has thirty times the population. Rihanna was also alone in a strange country far from home, but she stayed focused on her purpose. She says, "To pursue my dreams, and with their support, I left my entire family in Barbados to move to the States. It was a little scary to have no friends or family and all of a sudden step into a recording studio."[19]

She took it in stride. She claimed that when she left Barbados, she did not look back. She was willing to do whatever it took to be successful, even if it meant leaving her homeland and moving to another country. Yet there were many things she missed about Barbados:

> I loved hanging out with my two little brothers at the beach and hanging out with my friends at this club called The Boatyard. That was our spot, our thing. I loved it, the warm weather, the warm people, everyone there is more laid back. When I moved here everyone was more fast-paced about everything, it was completely different.[20]

When asked what her hardest adjustments were, she admits that she missed her family and friends. She also found the schools in the United States quite different. Eventually, because

Rihanna's move to New York City was overwhelming since it was larger than her entire island nation, with thirty times the population.

she needed to devote so much time to her music, she finished school with a private tutor.

The hours she put into her music paid off when Rogers and Sturken sent her demo tape around to studios. For many artists, waiting for music executives to review a demo tape and get back with an offer to audition can be a long process. Many companies do not respond at all. In Rihanna's case, though, offers soon came flooding in. Various companies requested auditions, but Def Jam, the first label to ask for a meeting, was the most enthusiastic.

The Next Step

For Rihanna, a chance to audition for the company that represented such famous musicians as Kanye West, Jay-Z, and Ne-Yo was the chance of a lifetime. It was also frightening. When she learned that she would be auditioning for Shawn Corey Carter, better known as Jay-Z, she was in awe. She had seen his picture on albums and in fan magazines, but the thought of actually performing in front of him was another story: "And that's when I really got nervous. I was like: 'Oh God, he's right there. I can't look, I can't look, I can't look!' I remember being extremely quiet. I was very shy. I was cold the entire time. I had butterflies. I'm sitting across from Jay-Z. Like, Jay-Zee.

I was star-struck."[21] Before she auditioned, however, Jay-Z put her at ease, and she was able to give the performance of her life. She sang Whitney Houston's "For the Love of Me" and two Sturken-Rogers compositions, "Pon De Replay" and "The Last Time."

Jay-Z

Born Shawn Corey Carter on December 4, 1969, Jay-Z took his stage name from his nickname, Jazzy. His name also comes from the J and Z subway lines in New York and is a tribute to Jaz-O, on whose albums he sang.

Abandoned by his father at age ten, Jay-Z grew up in the New York housing projects. One of his albums, *Can't Knock the Hustle*, tells of his drug dealing and hard childhood.

Jay-Z turned to music, but no recording companies picked up his first song. He formed his own company, Roc-A-Fella Records, with two friends in 1996. His career was launched when his album *Reasonable Doubt* made number twenty-three on the charts. Other bigger hits followed; so did seven Grammys.

Although he declared his retirement in 2003, he continued to perform. In 2005, at his famous "I Declare War" concert, he surprised the world by performing with his rival Nas. A statement he made later, after hearing criticism of hip-hop, explains his philosophy: "We have to respect each other's genre of music and move forward."

He was the chief executive officer of Def Jam from 2004 to 2008. He co-owns Rocawear clothing, the professional basketball team the New Jersey Nets, and a chain of sports bars, among other businesses. In 2007 he was the richest hip-hop artist in the country, worth about $940 million. On April 4, 2008, he married Beyoncé Knowles, and the two planned to launch a new label.

Quoted in Indo-Asian News Service, "Noel Gallagher Is Narrow Minded: Jay-Z," NDTV Music.com, May 13, 2008. www.ndtvmusic.com/story.asp?id=ENTEN20080049721.

Rihanna was star-struck when she first auditioned for music mogul Jay-Z. After she signed with his record label, the two of them—shown here with fellow Def Jam artist Teairra Mari (right)—formed a successful business partnership.

Signing on the Dotted Line

After she sang, she was startled when Jay-Z clapped for her performance. Then he let her know he was interested in having her as part of Def Jam. Jay-Z later admitted that it had only taken him two minutes to realize that Rihanna could be a star. He explains:

> It was in her eyes. She had it all in her eyes. The way she carried herself and performed right there on the spot, I was

like, "Wow, she's a star, we'll figure out the rest later." We wouldn't let her out of the building. We actually closed all the doors, brought her some food. She brought in her lawyers and her production team, and we signed the deal that day.[22]

He not only offered to sign her then and there, he offered her a six-album contract. He did not want to lose her to rival companies. Rihanna recalls that Def Jam locked her in their offices until 3 AM, and Jay-Z teased her that she had only two options for getting out: signing the papers or exiting through the window. Because they were on the twenty-ninth floor, Rihanna was flattered that he liked her singing that much.

For Rihanna to be signed by such a well-known label—and by none other than superstar Jay-Z himself—was incredible. "When Jay told me he wanted to sign me, I was smiling from ear to ear," she remembers. She agreed to the deal that night and signed the papers. "As I left Def Jam, I was walking up and down the streets screaming. I couldn't sleep for three nights straight. I woke up every second thinking is this for real?"[23]

The First Album

She soon realized she had a lot of work ahead of her. Rihanna, along with Rogers and Sturken, holed up in the New York studio to compose songs. Over the next few months, Rihanna recorded them, and her first album, *Music of the Sun*, came together. With its catchy beat and island cadence, it fused many Caribbean musical traditions and reflected the diversity of the Bajan language with its combination of British and West African speech.

Although Rihanna's homeland provided the inspiration, the true genius behind the success of the album was Syndicated Rhythm Productions. Rogers and Sturken did for her what they had done for other singers—put together a collection of tunes that showcased her unique talents. As critic Jason Birchmeier explains in the *All Music Guide*:

Rihanna benefits from the knowing production work of Syndicated Rhythm Productions, aka Evan Rogers and Carl Sturken. . . . What these guys do that's so irresistibly shrewd is synthesize Caribbean rhythms and beats with standard-issue urban dance-pop: Caribbean-inflected urban, if you will. So while a song like "Pon de Replay" . . . is driven by booming dancehall-lite beats and a reggae vocal cadence (and title spelling), it's a simple dance-pop song at its core, with . . . a can't-miss singalong hook (and a glitzy, urban-style MTV video to boot).[24]

Songwriters Evan Rogers (left) and Carl Sturken worked with Rihanna on her first hit songs.

Caribbean Music

Barbados was once a British colony, but its population has European, African, and South American roots. Thanks to this mix, the island has a variety of musical styles. One of the most popular is reggae, which has come to be associated with the Caribbean Islands. Reggae, which developed in Jamaica, is a blend of blues, calypso, and rock and roll. It has a strong, syncopated rhythm, and its lyrics are often protests against social injustice.

Another popular style is soca, dance music that originated in Trinidad and Tobago. It combines a strong, insistent percussion beat with lilting calypso music. It evolved from the local chutney music, which includes lyrics in Hindi or Bhojpuri (both languages from India) or in English, sung to an upbeat tempo. This music is usually accompanied by an Indian or Nepalese hand drum, a harmonium (a freestanding keyboard that sounds like an accordion), and metal rhythm sticks.

Rather than modeling her after other popular singers of the early 2000s—Alicia Keyes, Beyoncé Knowles, or Ashanti—they played up Rihanna's unique background. One advantage Rogers had was his knowledge of Barbados from his Bajan wife. He, like Rihanna, had absorbed the island rhythms. Rihanna's goal with her first album was to showcase her Caribbean heritage and reveal her fun side.

With that in mind, she helped write some of the songs. Many people wondered how much input Rihanna, as a sixteen-year-old, had in the creation of her albums. When Chris Rolls of MP3.com posed that question to her a year later, after her second album came out, Rihanna replied:

A good amount actually . . . as much as I want, really. But I don't like to be too much in control and too dominant. I like to hear other people . . . because I respect other people's opinion[s], especially in the creative world. . . . I get advice from producers . . . sometimes we go back and forth trying to figure out what's best and sometimes we just collaborate and make it the best.[25]

Relying on the judgment of pros like Rogers and Sturken proved to be a wise move. They had written "Pon de Replay," one of the tunes she had sung at her Def Jam audition. The duo was convinced it would be a hit, but Rihanna confessed, "Actually, when I first heard that song, I didn't want to do it, because it was very sing-songy and very—whatever. Nursery-rhymish. But after I started recording it, I went along with it and started liking it."[26]

To stir up interest in the album, "Pon de Replay" was released as a single in July 2005. The title is Caribbean slang meaning "play it again." And DJs around the country responded by doing just that.

Chapter 3

Topping
the Charts

Keeping a star popular often depends on timing. With so many singers vying for a place on the charts, a performer is only as good as his or her latest song. If too much time passes before a new song comes out, people can easily forget a former favorite. Before Rihanna's wave of popularity could crash onto the shore and recede, Def Jam wanted her riding the crest again. She needed to make a splash with her first album, then swiftly move on to her next.

On the Replay

"Pon de Replay" became one of the most played songs of summer 2005. It climbed the charts to number two on the *Billboard* Hot 100. Critics raved about Rihanna. Reviewer Justin Lewis described her debut in *Associated Content*:

> She blasted onto the scene and straight to the top of the charts with her energetic ode to dancehall grooving, "Pon De Replay." The infectious beat pulsating out your speakers and straight down your spine; Rihanna's accented soprano sounding hypnotic against the groove and burning the catchy hookline into your brain.[27]

Little X directed Rihanna's first video. In it, she electrifies a dull dance club by moving enticingly like a belly dancer while she sings "Pon de Replay." The DJ turns up the music, and the previously bored crowd goes wild and dances along with Rihanna. The video, too, became a hit.

The Thrill of Stardom

The excitement "Pon de Replay" generated among the dancehall crowd was nothing compared to the delight it gave Rihanna to

Rihanna on tour promoting her first album, **Music of the Sun,** *in Germany, 2005.*

hear her song played on the radio. The first time she heard it, she was at the mall. "I was running up and down screaming, and people looked at me like I was crazy," she says. "But I didn't care. It was my song and there was no other feeling like it!"[28]

She was glad, too, that the music reflected her heritage. As she explained to one interviewer, "I feel so proud to see the Caribbean just getting put on the map and people really accepting and respecting our music."[29]

When her first single reached number two on the charts, Rihanna was exhilarated to learn that the number-one song, "We Belong Together," was by her idol, Mariah Carey. Coming in second to the singer she had admired and imitated since childhood was a breathtaking experience for the now seventeen-year-old.

Album Debut

The popularity of "Pon de Replay" had eager audiences around the world waiting for the album release. When *Music of the Sun* came out a few months later in August 2005, a close-up of Rihanna graced the cover. The face of the pretty Bajan teen, who had won a beauty contest the year before, gave the album another strong selling point. People flocked to buy the recording by this previously unknown singer.

At first some people were skeptical about the album and about Rihanna herself. Music critic Jason Birchmeier explains:

> Given the proliferation of young and beautiful urban dance-pop divas dominating the radio and music video airwaves in 2005, it initially was tempting to discount Rihanna as yet another Beyoncé-Ciara-Ashanti cash-in. But like her Def Jam labelmate Teairra Mari—another young and beautiful urban dance-pop diva who emerged out of nowhere in 2005—Rihanna is winsome rather than wannabe, thanks in no small part to her producers.[30]

Some of the album's popularity was due to its unusual blend of music. It contained everything from ballads to reggae. One of Rihanna's fanzines praised the variety and commented that "besides ripping traditional reggae tracks like a seasoned dancehall queen, the stunning 17-year-old Rihanna possesses a powerful singing voice that conjures up feelings and experiences way beyond her years."[31]

Reviews ranged from one oft-repeated criticism that the album lacked replay value, ingenuity, and rhythm to that of *Rolling Stone* magazine, which described the album as "a seductive mix of big-voiced R&B and souped-up island riddims—what Beyoncé might have sounded like if she had grown up in the West Indies and skipped the whole Destiny's Child thing."[32]

Although many critics cited the unevenness of the album, most agreed that it was a good first effort. Others, such as music critic Bruce Britt, were more effusive with their praise. Britt saw Rihanna's album as a springboard to greater future successes. In *BMI Music World*, he predicted:

> Rihanna is much more than a dance-floor diva, as her Def Jam Records debut album, *Music of the Sun*, attests. Tracks like "The Last Time," "Here I Go Again," and "Now I Know" showcase an agile voice that's grounded in pop, soul, gospel, and Caribbean traditions. . . . Her debut album was one of the most anticipated pop recordings of 2005. Judging from its impressive mix of Caribbean dance jams, funk rumpshakers, and soul ballads, *Music of the Sun* is the auspicious beginning of a high-flying career.[33]

Name Recognition

His assessment was right. With "Pon de Replay" fast catching on and *Music of the Sun* debuting at number ten, Rihanna had already made an impressive start. To increase sales for her first album, she went on tour, opening for pop singer Gwen Stefani from October to December 2005.

Soon people not only came to see Stefani, but they bought tickets because they wanted to hear Rihanna, too. Her fan base grew. One of the reasons for Rihanna's popularity was her willingness to sing her heart out: "I just go for it [in concert]. I know that they came to see me, so I have to give them my all and make the show worth it for them."[34]

Touring with Stefani did more than introduce Rihanna's name to the public and sell albums. It acquainted her with a new music style. "Coming from Barbados, I really hadn't heard that much rock music," she explains. "Touring with Gwen changed my perspective. So, when I was discussing this project [her second album] with L.A. Reid, Chairman of Island Def Jam Records, I made sure to say I want to experiment with some rock."[35]

Rock would be a new addition to a repertoire that, until now, had mainly included music she had listened to as she was growing up. As she explains, "I loved reggae music and I still do—Bob Marley, of course, Sizzla, Sean Paul, Damian Marley. The vibe of

Touring with pop singer Gwen Stefani, pictured, allowed Rihanna to share her music with a larger audience.

Gwen Stefani

American singer Gwen Stefani struggled to stardom with her brother's group, No Doubt. The band's early releases were unsuccessful. In the early 1990s its ska-pop sound was not popular with fans of grunge. The band also went through rough times after the suicide of lead singer John Spence.

Stefani's failed romance with bandmate Tony Kanal almost broke up the band, but later it provided songs for the group's next album, *Tragic Kingdom*, in 1995. The tour for the album continued for more than two years. *Tragic Kingdom* sold more than 16 million copies worldwide and received Grammy nominations.

Even after that success, No Doubt's next album was poorly received. The group made a comeback with *Rock Steady* in 2001. This time it changed its sound to include dancehall and reggae, but it still kept some New Wave influences. "Hey Baby" and "Underneath It All," songs from the album, received Grammy Awards.

Stefani went solo with albums *Love. Angel. Music. Baby* (2004) and *The Sweet Escape* (2006), which garnered her Grammy Award nominations. "Hollaback Girl" became her first U.S. number-one single and the first digital download to reach more than 1 million in sales. Stefani is also known for her clothing line, L.A.M.B., a mix of ethnic styles from around the world.

---

it, that's what I love. It just makes you feel good. Reggae music is the music that I party to the most."[36] Now, however, she was ready to branch out in new directions as she started her next album.

Riding the Wave

Most companies wait at least a year before issuing a singer's next album, but Def Jam planned to release Rihanna's second album eight months after the first. Some reviewers saw the swift arrival of the second album as a cover-up for poor sales on the first one. Justin Lewis asks in *Associated Content*:

> So what does one do when their debut single is a smash hit and their debut album is lost in the shuffle in less than 6 months time? Go for the jugular, of course; call up some higher-profile producers, dilute the reggae with more straightlaced pop and R&B, send the artist's image into glamour overload, and issue forth a sophomore set in enough time to promote it as if your debut never really existed. And thus, 9 months after she emerged with *Music of the Sun*, Rihanna has returned to re-introduce herself with *A Girl Like Me*.[37]

Jay-Z contradicted that by saying that because Rihanna was a new artist, he wanted to get her music out to a wider audience. As part of that strategy, Def Jam planned to release a single from the album to start the publicity buzz. The first cut she recorded was "S.O.S." Rihanna loved the song's rebel sound and was eager to work on it. Three days later, she had finished the recording. Luckily for Rihanna, she was a hard worker and her motivation remained high. The time pressure to get a second album out so soon after the first one was intense. "S.O.S." was not the only song to be finished in record time.

Crazy Hours

While recording *A Girl Like Me*, Rihanna worked around a hectic schedule that included tours and interviews. She recalls:

> Unlike the first album, where we had three months set aside to get the album recorded, the second album, we had no time. We were still promoting the first album, still promoting the first singles, and we just had to fit it in where we could, like at the end of the day, like at 11:30 at night we would start recording. Producers had to fly all over the world and come record with me and work with me. . . . It was crazy. . . . We got it done, but I'm still amazed because we had no time.[38]

Rihanna filming the video for "S.O.S."

Her schedule throughout 2005 included waking at five o'clock in the morning to start rehearsals. Throughout the day she squeezed in time to do her schoolwork, give interviews, work on video shoots, and write and record songs. If she had expected stardom to be glamorous, she soon found out that it involved a lot of hard work. Her perception of what it meant to be a star altered. As she explained to one reporter, "My love for music and singing will never change, but the rose-colored glasses are no longer so rosy."[39]

More Personal

A life that looked alluring to outsiders was not as impressive to live. One of the most difficult adjustments for Rihanna was handling the many demands of her new lifestyle without the support of family and friends. She had little time to make new friends in New York or to reconnect with old ones. Instead, she poured these feelings into her songs:

> Many times over the past year, I didn't have anyone my age with me. When recording this album, I wanted it to seem like I was having a personal conversation with girls my age. People think, because we're young, we aren't complex, but that's not true. We deal with life and love and broken hearts in the same way a woman a few years older might. My goal on *A Girl Like Me* was to find songs that express the many things young women want to say, but might not know how.[40]

Most of the songs on the album dealt with personal issues Rihanna had faced. For example, "S.O.S." is about a crush. According to Rihanna, she chose this song because she had strong feelings about a guy that she wanted to overcome. With its subtitle, "Rescue Me," the song is a heartfelt plea for someone to save her from this obsession.

Popular with fans, "S.O.S." found its way into three music videos. One of them reached number one on MTV's *Total Request Live* and stayed there for almost three weeks. In it, Rihanna, wearing a bikini, calls for help on her cell phone. She listens to "Pon de Replay" and "Tainted Love"—the song from Soft Cell that inspired "S.O.S."

Added Exposure

Another of the three videos gave Rihanna international publicity: a Nike promotional video with "S.O.S." as the theme song. That video, centered around a dance contest in a gym, was Rihanna's first endorsement deal. Making the commercial gave her the opportunity to work with Jamie King, a choreographer who had also worked with stars such as Madonna and Shakira. During the six days it took to shoot the video, Rihanna learned a great deal about dance techniques. She disliked lunch breaks because she preferred to keep dancing.

The added exposure from the videos propelled "S.O.S." up the charts. It became Rihanna's first number-one hit on the Hot 100 chart. It also debuted at number one on the Hot Digital Songs chart and reached number one in Australia and number two in the United Kingdom.

Doing videos and promotional deals meant longer days in the studio, but Rihanna had inherited her mother's drive and ambition: "I just try to work hard. . . . I try to be a workaholic and try to do the best I can to get better,"[41] she says. Her goal is always to improve. She never wants to get comfortable with her level of success; instead, she plans to work harder to reach the next stage in her career.

Working with Stars

Moving to the next level included recording with several well-known singers and producers. To record her Yardie (Jamaican street gang) duet, "Break It Off," with Sean Paul, Rihanna flew to Jamaica. She enjoyed the time she spent with the DJ and Grammy Award-winning vocalist. "I have so much respect and love for Sean Paul. He took me to visit the Bob Marley Museum before going into the studio, which was an amazing experience. When we finally got to the studio, I felt as though Marley's spirit was in the room with us."[42]

Rihanna has performed on occasion with singer Ne-Yo. Here they sing together at the 2007 American Music Awards.

Another singer and songwriter she admired was Ne-Yo. After hearing "Let Me Love You," which Ne-Yo had written for R&B and pop singer Mario's second album, Rihanna decided she wanted to work with Ne-Yo. She explains, "For the second album, I was like, 'You know what? I have to work with that guy Ne-Yo.' And it made it a lot easier because he's on the same

Ne-Yo

Grammy Award-winning vocalist and songwriter Shaffer Chimere Smith, born October 18, 1982, took the stage name Ne-Yo. His first album, *In My Own Words* (2006), debuted at number one on the *Billboard* 200. More than three hundred thousand copies sold the first week, and it was certified platinum. *Because of You* (2007), his second album, also went platinum. His third, *Year of the Gentleman*, came out in 2008.

Ne-Yo's work is known for its appeal to people of all ages and backgrounds. This is something he strives to achieve; he has traveled the world and wants to include those experiences in his music.

In addition to songs for his own album, Ne-Yo has written for Whitney Houston, Jennifer Hudson, Janet Jackson, Mary J. Blige, Britney Spears, and Celine Dion, among others. He is also known for the Grammy-nominated song "Irreplaceable" that he wrote for Beyoncé.

When asked how he comes up with his ideas, he explains, "Sometimes I see a picture in a magazine, a painting in a museum, or a word on a page, and that's all I need to trigger the thoughts." He also claims that growing up in a house full of females gave him insight into writing songs for women.

In 2007 he opened his own recording studio, Carrington House. Paula Campbell, Sixx John, and Shanell were the first to sign with his label, Compound Entertainment.

Quoted in Def Jam Recordings, "Ne-Yo: Biography," 2008. www.defjam.com/site/artist_bio.php?artist_id=593.

label I am. So we went into the studio and we started working on this song 'Unfaithful.' And it's one of my favorite songs on the album."[43]

"Unfaithful," a song about a girl cheating on her boyfriend, struck a chord with audiences everywhere when it was released as a single. Songs have often been written about guys cheating on their girlfriends, but Rihanna wanted to turn the tables. She says, "On a lot of records, men talk about cheating as though it's all a game. For me, 'Unfaithful' is not just about stepping out on your man, but the pain that it causes both parties."[44]

Rihanna felt sure the song would be a hit. Def Jam decided to release "Unfaithful" as the album's second single. Putting it out as a single was risky because it was the first time she had done a stand-alone ballad.

Some fans who loved "S.O.S." enjoyed Rihanna's new sound. Others, however, did not appreciate the change of style. After it came out in July 2006, one reviewer commented:

> Is this really the same Rihanna who took the charts by storm with "S.O.S," that electro-pop-tastic take on "Tainted Love"? Regrettably, yes—this overwrought ballad smacks of cynicism, an attempt to keep all the usual album-filling bases covered rather than develop the upbeat style which clearly suits Rihanna so much better. Plinky piano melodies, plasticky strings, and hilariously melodramatic lyrics add up to one very disappointing single.[45]

In spite of the criticism, "Unfaithful," like "S.O.S.," rose to the top of the charts. Rihanna soon found herself at number one again.

A Change of Pace

The ballad was not the only different sound on the album. Gwen Stefani's influence was obvious in some songs. Rihanna wanted to meld rock with reggae. She used this new combination in the song "Kisses Don't Lie."

She was pleased with the new sound as well as the variety on her album. More importantly, she felt that everything on the album revealed "what it's like to be a girl like me. Whether I'm cheating on people, whether I've been cheated on, falling in and out of love, people hating on me, having that crazy feeling that guys give you, partying—every aspect of my life."[46] The music was not so much about her culture as it was about her. The songs on the album, some of which she cowrote, were much more personal this time.

The Sophomore Album

Rihanna had shared herself and her deeper feelings in the singles that came out, and most fans loved her openness. Capitalizing on these successes, Def Jam released the second album in April

Rihanna speaks at a press conference in Barbados about the release of her second album, A Girl Like Me, in 2006.

The Pussycat Dolls

The Pussycat Dolls began in a small dance studio in actress Christina Applegate's garage. Her roommate, Robin Antin, invited a few dancer friends to join her, and they played around with different moves. Antin describes her motive behind starting the group: "Inside every woman is a Pussycat Doll. It's about female empowerment, about being confident with who you are. It's about singing and dancing in front of a mirror by yourself and having fun."

They began by performing at Johnny Depp's club, the famous Viper Room on Sunset Strip in California, where they became the opening act once a week for six years. In 2000 Gwen Stefani offered to perform and sing with them. Christina Aguilera did, too. By 2002 the group had moved to a bigger club.

Their first album, *PCD*, sold four million copies worldwide. Two of their songs were number-one hits—"Don't Cha" and "Stickwitu." They also had two top-three singles—"Beep" and "Buttons." By the time Rihanna joined them on tour in 2006, they had become the biggest girl band in the world.

Quoted in Pussycat Dolls, "Bio," 2007. www.pcdmusic.com//Main.aspx?pbt_name=Bio.

2006. To promote it, Rihanna went on tour that fall. She opened for the Pussycat Dolls, an award-winning, all-girl band.

Whereas reviews on the first album had been mixed, this one met with mainly praise. In a review written before the album hit the stores, Chris Rolls of MP3.com concluded:

It seems like the winter was just not cold enough to chill the fiery Caribbean breeze that Rihanna generated last summer. In fact, it has been less than a year since Rihanna's *Music of the Sun* delivered the scorching dance floor hit "Pon de Replay." This summer may prove to be another one spent sweating to Rihanna with the release of her latest album, *A Girl Like Me*.[47]

With the debut of her sophomore album, Rihanna established herself in the music world. In addition to talent, her success thus far had been fueled by hard work and determination. She would need plenty more of both to face the many challenges that stardom brought.

Chapter 4

Lonely at the Top

Videos, tours, and media interviews kept Rihanna in the spotlight from 2006 on. Glamour magazines splashed her face across magazine covers. She danced her way across television screens in a Nike ad to the music of "S.O.S." JCPenney offered her an endorsement deal. She had a cameo appearance in the film *Bring It On: All or Nothing*, and she performed some of her songs in episodes of *Las Vegas* and *All My Children*.

Accolades flowed in, including Teen Choice Awards for Female Breakout Artist and Choice R&B Artist, a MuchMusic Video Award for Best International Artist, and an MTV Video Music Award from Japan. Her homeland honored her in eight categories at the Barbados Music Awards. Rihanna was living her dream of making music all over the world.

Autograph Seekers

Fans recognized her when she was out in public. They clamored for autographs. The first time it happened, she admits, "It felt so good and weird. They were even apologizing and said, 'Sorry to bother you but can I please have your autograph,' and I'm like, Don't apologize, I want to give you my autograph."[48] Another time, she recalls:

> I was at [an ice cream shop] one day and there was this flock of children, maybe 16 of them, and they all started grabbing

napkins and they were like, "Can I have an autograph *pleeease*?" That was a moment for me because I used to be in that position. I would see a star and just beg for their autograph. And then for people to be asking me, I felt honored.[49]

Writing so many signatures meant she had to learn to do them quickly. At first, she spent a lot of time practicing a simpler version of her autograph. Others warned her that when crowds began shoving pens and paper at her, she would need to rush

Rihanna makes time to sign autographs for children at a benefit concert for her "Believe" charity, 2008.

through it. She would have little time to write her usual, careful signature. Rihanna soon put her newfound skill into practice. Everywhere she went, people pleaded for her autograph.

Phony Friends

As a new star, Rihanna faced another problem as well. Many people are eager to befriend a celebrity. Rihanna quickly learned to tell the genuine from the false. She says, "I'm very good at figuring out who is real and which people want to be my friend because of what I am versus who I am."[50]

She had an advantage, however. From the time Rihanna was young, she had studied the people around her. "I have always had a thing for reading people," she reveals. "When I come into contact with a situation or a person, the first thing I do is, I'm

Beyoncé, Jay-Z, and Rihanna

One rumor floating around after *A Girl Like Me* came out was that Jay-Z was romantically involved with Rihanna. The two of them had been spending a lot of time together. When reporters asked her about it, Rihanna said it was because they were both with the same record label.

Gossip increased when Beyoncé released "Ring the Alarm." Many people thought the lyrics—featuring a woman ranting because her man had cheated on her—expressed Beyoncé's rage at Jay-Z for taking up with Rihanna. When an interviewer suggested Beyoncé had been brave for putting out that song, Beyoncé replied, "To be honest with you, I didn't really hear those rumors. When things are not true, you really don't think about it, you know what I mean? You're not scared of it because it's not true." Much of the gossip was silenced when Jay-Z married Beyoncé on April 4, 2008.

Quoted in Holly Eagleson, "Beyoncé," *Seventeen*, January 2007, p. 70.

just quiet for a little while. I sit, I watch you, I observe you. And being able to read people helps me to know how easy it is to be read. I know the key things that show people who you are."[51]

Rihanna discovered that success had its pros and cons. Being popular brought many benefits, but it was often difficult to know whom to trust. She found she must always be on guard because people sometimes put on fronts or pretend to be different than they really are. One of her greatest disappointments was finding out that many people connected with show business are both shallow and dishonest.

Rihanna's fanzines emphasize her preference for people who are honest and loyal. True friends like that are hard to find. When celebrities have friends, constant travel and long hours make it difficult to keep in touch. Because her tours and performances take her all over the world, Rihanna is often in a different time zone from her friends, so she is not able to call them after a performance. Although she accepts that as part of the life she has chosen, it is not always easy.

The Dark Side of Success

Most of the time Rihanna is surrounded by adoring fans and numerous production people. Yet as she confided to reporter Dan Cairns of the *Sunday Times*, the reality is not what most people think. Few people realize the loneliness she faces:

> At first, I was on an adrenaline high: this is my dream, I'm actually doing it. It didn't phase [faze] me that I was alone, that I wasn't with the people I love. But after a while it gets repetitive, and that's when you kind of go, "Oh, wow, I'm sitting in a hotel room once again, me and the television." When you're in the spotlight, people are like, "What do you have to worry about?" They forget that the success is one great aspect of your life, but behind that there are problems, there are dark sides, there's loneliness, unhappiness.[52]

Exhaustion sets in, too, as performers move from one city to another to put on shows. "Artists work so hard and the people around them keep pushing, forgetting they're human," Rihanna explains. "And in turn the artist also forgets she's human and stops caring—and that's when you get lonely."[53] Performers who are lonely and tired often try to find something to fill the emptiness, sometimes with dangerous results.

Filling the Void

Some of Rihanna's peers, who rose to fame as quickly as she did, turned to drugs for comfort. Later, they struggled to overcome addictions. Rihanna understands their reasons for taking drugs but insists she would never do drugs herself. She has seen first-hand the devastation drug addiction brings.

Growing up with a father who struggled to overcome his crack addiction taught her to avoid drugs. She has assured many interviewers that she would never go down that path because she knows the problems taking drugs can bring. Knowing how much pain it caused her own family, she vowed she would never put herself in that situation.

Like many other stars, Rihanna, too, has experienced the loneliness and the demands that come with being famous. Yet rather than cracking under pressure, she says she thrives on it. She also believes it is important to stay focused and not let stardom go to her head. She credits the support from her family and friends as crucial in keeping her stable. "I keep good people around me," Rihanna says. "My best friends are always there for me. They're honest and they keep me in check."[54]

Feet on the Ground

Stardom occurred so quickly that Rihanna was stunned. When her music started to take off, it reminded her of a whirlwind. Caught in the middle, she watched it all swirl around her. As if she were in the calm eye of the hurricane, nothing affected her at first. She had trouble convincing herself it was real:

It is crazy because I see everything happening but none of it's really hitting me. It's so weird because everybody calls me [and says], "Your song is number one," and I'm like, "Thank you!" But I'm still in shock, I still haven't, like,

Rihanna credits her relationships with her friends for keeping her grounded.

Something from Nothing?

Although Rihanna has insisted her male companions are only friends, the media love to speculate. One evening the press spotted her and actor Shia LaBeouf having dinner in a restaurant. The reporters admitted that the pair did not hold hands or kiss, but they labeled it a romantic dinner because it ended with strawberries and champagne. The article also indicated that, because the dinner lasted so long, the two must be dating.

The media also linked Rihanna's name with Josh Hartnett. When one Web site posted quotes purportedly given by Rihanna, another site tried to set the record straight:

> This is the fake quote Rihanna supposedly gave at the World Music Awards in Monte Carlo last weekend: "I would be lying if I told you [Josh and I] were not more than just friends. I have so fallen for him, he is lovely. He is so hot and he is really sweet to me. When we hang out it feels right—even though it's still pretty new."
>
> Rihanna says, "That is completely incorrect. People quote me on things that I never said. That quote is not a real quote. It's not right at all."

Just Jared.com, "Rihanna: For the Last Time, I Am Not Dating Josh Hartnett," November 13, 2007. http://justjared.buzznet.com/2007/11/13/rihanna-dating-josh-hartnett/.

really freaked out and thought, "Oh my gosh, my song is number one." I'm still trying to make myself freak out. If you have the number one song in the country, you should be smiling every second.[55]

Reality gradually set in, and Rihanna needed her friends more than ever. She has a group of loyal friends who help to keep her grounded and prevent her from getting conceited. "It comes from my upbringing in Barbados," she explains. She and her friends would laugh at imitations of each other all the time. "It's almost second nature to us that we don't let each other get above ourselves."[56]

With her friends' help, she hopes never to get arrogant or pushy. Some celebrities turn into divas with arrogant attitudes, and they expect people to cater to their whims. Rihanna, though, believes it is important to be gracious and to treat others kindly. That includes the media, the people she works with, and her fans.

Playing the Game

Rihanna also knows that audiences expect her always to be at her best. She understands the importance of being upbeat, so she tries hard to be friendly even when she is tired or depressed. Sometimes she struggles to be cheerful:

> I love what I do but, yes, this stuff does start to take its toll on you. Sometimes you get really miserable and on the edge, but people don't know why you're acting like that. You always want to be kind to people, so you're forced to be a bubbly person, but, to be honest, sometimes I'd just like to sit in a corner by myself and be quiet.[57]

She never does; instead, she continues to play the part people expect of her. She developed a reputation for being charming to both interviewers and fans. Yet many stars who start out charming end up as divas. Some reporters wondered if Rihanna would fall into this common trap as her popularity increased.

Maureen Paton of *You* magazine describes the reactions when Rihanna did not show up on time for an interview:

> Everyone is in a tizzy because Rihanna is late. Poised with their cosmetic weapons of mass construction, the assembled hairdressers and stylists exchange significant looks. There's usually only one reason in the pampered world of show business why a star shows up late. Delusions of divadom, right?

> Wrong, in Rihanna's case.[58]

Her lateness was not due to attitude; she had a genuine emergency. The crew realized they were mistaken when Rihanna showed up at the studio with her foot in a cast. Rihanna had broken her toe. Paton characterized the singer as humble and cheerful throughout the interview.

Strict Standards

Rihanna's high expectations for herself show not only in her day-to-day dealings with others but also in her work ethic. She is grateful for her success and is determined that stardom will not change her standards. Being polite and kind to others is one of her values; remaining drug-free is another.

Rihanna claims there is one additional line she will never cross due to the strict moral standards of her Bajan home. Early in her career she was adamant that she would never bare her body in public. Her mother had raised her with certain values. She insists, "My mother would kill me if I posed nude!"[59]

Maintaining those expectations in the face of career pressures will not be easy. Yet Rihanna believes she has the strength of character and the determination to weather the storms that come her way. Nowhere was that more evident than in the planning for her next release, "Umbrella."

New Image

As Rihanna's confidence grew, she no longer was content to let others tell her what to do or stage-manage the persona she presented to the public. Until early 2007 she sang songs that others suggested. She also acquiesced to their ideas of how she should look. Though she longed to try new things, she was pressured to maintain the same image.

Rihanna first asserted herself while she was on tour in Europe to promote her second album, *A Girl Like Me*. She went into a beauty salon in Paris, where they cut her long hair into a stylish, chin-length bob. She loved her new look, but she ran into difficulties as soon as she returned to her hotel. Some people complimented her on the haircut, but others insisted she needed

Rihanna understands the importance of being upbeat at all times with her fans, such as when she appeared on MTV's TRL in 2008.

Under the Umbrella

"**U**mbrella" had originally been written for Britney Spears, but her people turned it down. Next, the songwriters offered it to Mary J. Blige and Def Jam. Soon the two companies were engaged in a bidding war. According to Tricky Stewart, one of the song's producers, they had intended to wait until they heard from Blige because she had been nominated for eight Grammys.

Rihanna determined that she wanted that song with its island lilt. She claims she cornered one of the songwriters and begged to record the tune. Def Jam persisted until Stewart gave in.

Stewart did not think Rihanna was the right person to sing "Umbrella," but he changed his mind after she recorded the "ellas" in the refrain. "You knew it was about to be the jump-off," he says, "and your life was about to change if you had anything to do with that record." After Jay-Z added a verse and performed the rap, the rest was history.

Quoted in Maureen Paton, "The Dark Secret in Raunchy Pop Sensation Rihanna's Past," *You*, November 2007. www.dailymail.co.uk/you/article-492706/The-dark-secret-raunchy-pop-sensation-Rihannas-past.html.

to return her hair to its original look. Rihanna gave in and had hair extensions put in. She recalls:

> It just crushed me. When you're growing up, 17, 18, that's when you're really trying to figure out who you are, and at that point I just wanted to try something outside of the box. But as soon as you come out of your shell, like, "This is who I am," they just shove you back in with, "No, because this is what we want the box to look like."[60]

She preferred her edgier new look, but she yielded to studio pressure to return to her original image. As she matured, though, she realized that the image they were asking her to project was not the person she was inside. Once she understood that, she

Rihanna teamed up with director Chris Applebaum, pictured, to shoot a daring video for her song "Umbrella," and the resulting success included the Best Video award at the MTV Video Music Awards in 2007.

rebelled: "I felt like the whole world had long, curly blonde hair. Ciara, Beyoncé, Mariah, Christina Milian. Everybody wanted to be like everybody else. So I cut my hair. . . . The second time, I didn't have any discussions, nothing. I just cut it, I dyed it black, and I went into the studio making music my way."[61]

This new, feisty spirit showed through as she began her next project. When she recorded *Good Girl Gone Bad*, her third album, she decided to take more chances not just with her appearance but in her music and videos, too.

To launch "Umbrella," her first single from the album, Rihanna contacted Chris Applebaum, who had directed videos for Hilary Duff, Britney Spears, and Madonna. She asked him to send her something extraordinary that included choreography. She was quite specific that she wanted this video to be unusual and different from others she had done.

Applebaum was up to the challenge. He came up with a proposal for her video, but he was uncertain how Rihanna would respond to his creative ideas. One suggestion in particular would be a big leap.

Taking Chances

Applebaum presented his vision to Rihanna. At the end of the video, he wanted her to look like a classic Greek statue—wearing nothing but silver body paint. He explained that during that portion of the video, she would no longer be herself; instead, she would be portraying her alter ego. Applebaum sent out the proposal and followed up with a phone call a few days later to see if she was willing to do it."[62] To his surprise and delight, Rihanna said yes.

Her answer proved Applebaum's theory about her: "There's greatness about her," he says. "Greatness as an artist, as a performer, as a person. There's something about her that's so inspiring, as an artist, she's unclassifiable. . . . She's more of an impresario."[63]

With only one day to shoot the video, the pressure was incredible, and Applebaum admitted to feeling stressed. Rihanna had to be repainted between each take to ensure that she was completely covered with silver. As she curled up and flowed from one position to the next, camera angles obscured her private parts from view. The graceful moves emphasized the artistry of the choreography.

The elegance and beauty of the scene stunned Applebaum's assistant. With tears in her eyes, she exclaimed, "This is the most incredible thing I've ever seen."[64] Applebaum agreed that the video they had just shot was magnificent.

Mixed Reactions

Audiences were stunned when Rihanna appeared in the final segment of the "Umbrella" video in nothing but silver paint. Though no one could argue with the beauty of the finished product, some people questioned her decision, given her strong past statements about nudity. She responded to one interviewer, "When I did that metallic body paint stuff for my 'Umbrella' video, I didn't do it to show my body. I didn't do it for people to like me. I did it because it was a cool visual, unexpected, and it looked hot."[65] The intention of that segment was for her to look arty rather than suggestive.

Many Bajans, however, were upset about the suggestiveness of photos and videos promoting Rihanna's music. Maureen Paton notes in an interview with Rihanna: "The foxy new look hasn't gone down well with everyone back home in Barbados. . . . Despite its laid-back air, the Caribbean is still a God-fearing, church-going part of the world."[66] Rihanna agreed that many Bajans were shocked by her new image. She faced a great deal of criticism about her clothing and behavior, especially from older people on the island, who tended to be conservative and judgmental.

It bothered Rihanna that "they always have something to say about what I'm wearing, what I'm not wearing, like in the 'Umbrella' video. If I wear a swimsuit on the beach, it's a problem; they put it on the front of the newspaper and call into programs."[67] But she was not about to let the negative publicity affect her. She understands that there will always be people who disapprove of what she does, but she tries to concentrate on those around her

Rihanna performs "Umbrella" at the MTV Movie Awards Show in 2007.

who are positive, such as her family and friends who support and encourage her.

A Transformation

Rihanna's new vision was to be herself, to ignore other people's ideas of what was right for her, and to do what reflected her inner self. She chose her third album title with that in mind.

I was embarking on a whole new image, a whole new journey. I wanted to differentiate myself from the past. I have come into my own and I know what I'm doing now. I've called the new album *Good Girl Gone Bad* because I was determined to do it my way. I was sick of listening to what everyone else wanted. This is the way I like to look and sound, so I became very rebellious—that's the attitude of the entire project."[68]

"Umbrella" was only the start of her changed appearance and sound. With *Good Girl Gone Bad*, no longer would she be one person on the inside and another on the outside. She wanted her stage image to match her inner self. Her only worry now was whether audiences would be as enthusiastic about the change as she was.

Chapter 5

Awards
Rain Down

A long with her music fame, Rihanna signed endorsement contracts. Gillette paid her to advertise its Venus Breeze razors. She also became the face for CoverGirl cosmetics. The Bajan tomboy now appeared in glamour magazines around the world in various states of dress or undress. She developed her signature look, fingernails, and fan base—all necessary components of stardom. She climbed toward the pinnacle, however, when she received several Grammy nominations in December 2007. Was it possible that newcomer Rihanna could compete against the big names in the music world and win one of the top awards in the industry?

Stormy Weather

The road to the summit of stardom started out wet. When Rihanna's single "Umbrella" hit the stores in England during May 2007, a deluge stuck. Never in the past two hundred years had the country seen such a downpour. Umbrellas popped open everywhere, both indoors and out. Capitalizing on the situation, the Totes company came out with a Rihanna umbrella. The soggy weather and the sea of umbrellas formed the perfect backdrop for Rihanna's latest hit.

Whether it was the rain or the combination of the Rihanna/ Jay-Z vocals, the song stayed at the number one position in the United Kingdom for ten weeks. In the United States, it soared from number forty-one to number one, where it remained for seven weeks. The "Umbrella" video had an equally impressive debut at number ten on MTV's *Total Request Live*. It rose to number one within a week and held that position for fifteen days, the longest of any video released in 2007. YouTube viewers watched it more than nine million times.

The rain lasted so long that some newspapers called it the "Rihanna Curse" and jokingly blamed her fans, saying they were doing rain dances to "Umbrella." Interestingly enough, the U.K. storms cleared after Timbaland's "The Way I Are" overtook "Umbrella" for the number-one spot. Storms also plagued the New Zealand, Spain, and Greek releases. In spite of the weather,

One of Rihanna's endorsement contracts was with makeup giant CoverGirl.

both the song and video reached the top ten in many countries around the world and stayed there that summer.

Weathering the Storm

As the song's popularity spread, rumors about Rihanna and Jay-Z's relationship circulated. The "Umbrella" lyrics led people to wonder if Rihanna and Jay-Z were only singing (and later acting in the video) or if they truly did care for each other as the song indicated. Rihanna agreed that "Umbrella" was a song about a relationship, but she pointed out that it could be about friendship as well as romance. She had chosen to sing it because she wanted to do something different, something that people would not expect from her. The many hours she had spent with Jay-Z, she insisted, had been time spent working on the song, not developing a relationship.

Rihanna and Jay-Z in concert together in 2008. Rihanna had to quash rumors about her relationship with Jay-Z, insisting that the two were not romantically involved.

In spite of Rihanna's denials, the media persisted in linking her name with Jay-Z's. Some people suggested that Rihanna was trying to unseat Beyoncé in both the music world and with her boyfriend, Jay-Z. Rihanna denied that and said that she admired Beyoncé and viewed her as a role model. She classified herself as Jay-Z's new protégée, and she viewed Beyoncé as a celebrity and a seasoned performer, someone she aspired to be like. Rihanna did admit that she hoped to reach the same heights as Jay-Z's girlfriend someday, but she made it clear, "I'm not looking to steal [Beyoncé's] crown. I'm looking to get my own."[69]

In Demand

With "Umbrella," she was well on her way. A flurry of requests for interviews, photo shoots, and endorsement deals soon followed. Magazines such as *Teen Vogue*, *InStyle*, *Allure*, *You*, and *FHM* vied for her time. The young, naïve Rihanna, with her long tresses and her gentle Caribbean manners, set about transforming herself into a sexy, sultry temptress as she appeared on the covers of more than thirty fashion publications, including *Glamour*, *Seventeen*, *Complex*, and *Giant*.

She shed the sweet, feminine image her producers had chosen and became, according to *InStyle* magazine, a "trendsetter with neon nails, spiky locks, and a love of experimentation."[70] Tattoos, huge earrings, and Christian Louboutin shoes became part of her signature style. The one-time tomboy transformed herself into a fashion icon.

Once she had been too shy to protest when her producers told her how to dress and what to wear, but she now asserted herself. She willingly let hairstylists and makeup artists experiment with her look, but she was not afraid to speak up if she did not like their ideas. Because she was the one who had to appear in public, she had the final say about what looked and felt right. Unlike most stars, she does not mind being seen without makeup. She was photographed for *People* magazine's "Most Beautiful" issue without it, and she insists she prefers the freedom and comfort of the natural look.

That attitude extends to her body as well. She says she will never have plastic surgery. She readily admits that the thought of the knife terrifies her, but, more importantly, she is content with her looks. "I like my body and I work out as hard as I can to make it as perfect as possible. But at the end of the day there's always people who criticise your weight, your hairstyle, and what you're wearing. I just get on with it."[71]

An Edgier Sound

Rihanna's newfound confidence showed in her music. Her first album showcased her island background; her second, her young teen persona; but her third became her breakout album. When she was working on it, she said that it expressed where she was in her life and in her career. Her goal was to break away from the innocent image that had been forced on her early in her career. She defined her new sound for interviewers, saying, "It's a lot edgier than the rest of the stuff that anyone has heard from me before. I'm singing about different things, it's a lot sexier."[72]

The album title, *Good Girl Gone Bad*, caused a stir in the media, and many people wondered what she meant by the phrase "Gone Bad." Rihanna explained to reporters that, to her, the word *bad* did not mean "sleazy." It only meant that she had become rebellious and had started taking risks. She then clarified her definition of the word bad: "Bad means cool, bad means funky, bad means having an attitude, bad means being edgy."[73]

Many people admired Rihanna's new look and sound. Talia Kraines of the British Broadcasting Corporation (BBC), for example, applauded the changes Rihanna had made on her latest album: "Three cheers for her declaration that 'once a good girl goes bad, she's gone forever.' If being bad does this for Rihanna, then being good, is like, totally overrated."[74]

Star-Studded Cast

Asserting herself paid off in other ways: Rihanna selected her collaborators for the album. She chose to work with Ne-Yo and Stargate again. She and Ne-Yo teamed up for "Hate That I Love

Rihanna at the screening of her third album, Good Girl Gone Bad, *2008. The album was edgier than her previous two albums.*

You," later released as a single. One reviewer praised this song, saying Rihanna's and Ne-Yo's "voices go together like strawberries and cream."[75] By contrast, many reviewers panned "Question Existing," the other song Rihanna and Ne-Yo did together, although most agreed Rihanna sang beautifully about the heartaches and loneliness of stardom.

New to this album were tracks by Justin Timberlake and Timbaland. Rihanna had always hoped to work with Timberlake. She got her wish one night after a show:

> Justin just came into the studio and he started messing around, making a beat. And it was fun. We played around with that one, too. And when we came to New York, Justin came back to the studio and he was like, "I wanna write this song for Rihanna." So Timbaland had an idea and he knew he wanted to call the song "Rehab" and he had a beat. So then Justin Timberlake . . . wrote the song in his head. He didn't write anything on paper. He went into the booth and sang it and I was very, very impressed. We all loved it.[76]

For Rihanna, working with Timberlake turned out to be fun. She admired his sense of humor but was impressed by his seri-

Rihanna performing with Justin Timberlake at the MTV Video Music Awards in 2007. In 2008 she collaborated with Timberlake on the song "Rehab."

Justin Timberlake

Pop singer and songwriter Justin Randall Timberlake was born on January 31, 1981, in Memphis, Tennessee. From 1993 to 1995, he was a member of *The Mickey Mouse Club*, along with Britney Spears and Christina Aguilera.

He started out as a lead singer in the band 'N Sync, but he later released his first solo album, *Justified*, in 2002. His next, *Future Sex/Love Sounds* came out in 2006. His first two albums sold more than 18 million copies.

Before he was allowed to receive the two awards he won at the 2004 Grammys, he had to apologize for the "wardrobe malfunction" that occurred during the Super Bowl. As part of the show, he had pulled off part of Janet Jackson's black leather outfit.

Timberlake has appeared in movies; has recorded songs with various performers, including Madonna and Rihanna; has opened several restaurants; has started a clothing line; and is the host of the Professional Golfers' Association tour. By 2008 he had won six Grammys, an Emmy, and three American Music Awards.

ousness about his work. She also enjoyed working with Timbaland. They added the catchy dance tune "Sell Me Candy" and the reggae-based song "Lemme Get That" to the album.

Rihanna admits that when she and Timberlake first recorded together, she was awestruck by being in the same room as him. The song they worked on together, "Rehab," was later released as a single. Reviewers praised the catchy ballad for its smooth instrumentals that fit perfectly with Rihanna's voice. Reviewer Jason Kennedy believed the romantic sound made "Rehab" a good choice for slow dances and predicted it would be played for years to come.

Timberlake hoped the ballad would show that Rihanna had hit a point in her career where the music world should see her as an adult. Jay-Z was equally impressed with Rihanna's latest sound. He told reporters, "She's found her voice. That's the best thing for any label—to have an artist step in and take control of their own career. She's left the nest."[77]

Conflicting Reviews

Not all critics were as effusive with their praise. AllHipHop.com wrote, "Now on her third album in as many years, Rihanna's challenge is proving that she's more than just a pretty girl being used to sell 'Urban' flavored bubblegum. Sadly for her, this album will do nothing to help her plight."[78]

Kari Livingston of *Associated Content* agreed. She indicated that not much on the album made it different from Rihanna's other two efforts. Livingston also complained that because the final track on the album was the mid-tempo song "Good Girl Gone Bad," the CD did not end on its strongest note.

Other reviewers disagreed. Talia Kraines of the BBC countered:

Rihanna and her team of famous songwriters and producers have grabbed some of the chunkiest beats from the 1990s and pulled off a stunning 3rd album that's packed full of singles. . . . The sizzling "Umbrella" might be the biggest hit Rihanna's ever had, but there's plenty on this album that could do even better.[79]

Portrait magazine concurred that Rihanna had produced a solid album. Its reviewers felt that *Good Girl Gone Bad* far surpassed her two earlier releases and predicted that it would spend all summer in many teens' mp3 players. Fans around the world must have agreed. *Good Girl Gone Bad* debuted at number two on the *Billboard* Top 200 and went triple platinum in Europe after its release in June 2007.

Award Winners

Three singles in addition to "Umbrella" hit the shelves during the summer of 2007. "Shut Up and Drive" made the top fifteen. "Hate That I Love You" and "Don't Stop the Music" both ended

The Grammy Awards

Originally called the Gramophone Awards, the Grammys got their name from the trophy given to outstanding musicians. The trophy is a miniature gold gramophone—an old-fashioned record player—on a stand. The Grammys began in 1958 to recognize artists; they are the music industry's highest honor. The first awards ceremony was held on May 4, 1959, in Beverly Hills, California.

The awards ceremony, now usually scheduled in February, has been broadcast on television since 1971. The most important categories are Record of the Year, Album of the Year, Song of the Year, and Best New Artist. Record companies and the National Academy of Recording Arts & Sciences, Inc., an organization of music professionals, choose the works they believe are the best from the past year. Members vote for the winner, but they can only vote in categories in which they are experts.

Some people have criticized the Grammys because they do not always reflect public opinion. Others believe they are a way for the recording industry to advertise. Most artists appreciate them for the recognition they bring. They find that winning a Grammy translates into much higher sales for the work.

up in the top ten. These singles put Rihanna in the running for major awards.

At the 2007 MTV Video Music Awards that fall, Rihanna was nominated for five awards, including Female Artist of the Year. When the winners were announced, she received two trophies— Video of the Year and Monster Single of the Year—for "Umbrella." Even more impressive, she had garnered six Grammy nominations for "Umbrella," "Don't Stop the Music," and "Hate That I Love You." The line-up of stars for that evening included most of Rihanna's childhood idols as well as many collaborators on her albums. Rihanna had to wait until February 2008 for her big night—the fiftieth Grammy Awards at the Staples Center in Los

Rihanna won a Grammy Award in 2008 for Best Rap/Sung Collaboration for "Umbrella."

Angeles, California—to find out if she would surpass them in any of the categories.

The Red-Carpet Stroll

Cameras flashed as Rihanna entered the Staples Center wearing a flirty, electric blue Zac Posen dress. The bling on her arm glittered. She had watched the Grammys before, but this time she was the center of attention. "I did what I thought I was supposed to do," she says, "because I'd seen other people do it. I knew that on the red carpet, you stop and you shake and you smile. But you don't really know. Everybody's calling your name—that was weird to me. And I thought I wasn't pleasing them. They all sounded so angry: 'Rihanna, look here'; 'No, look *here*, Rihanna.'"[80]

Time after time the media captured her pose. Fans pushed each other aside for a glimpse as she strolled down the famed red carpet. Attending the Grammy Awards that evening is a memory she will never forget. The highlight of the evening was the announcement of Best Rap/Sung Collaboration: "Umbrella" won.

When they called her name, Rihanna hugged Jay-Z and then headed to the stage to receive her award. She had promised to give her father her first Grammy, but, at the microphone, she told him they would have to fight over who got to keep it. After thanking all the people who had helped her, including Jay-Z and her family, she held her Grammy high as she exclaimed, "Barbados, I love you! We got one!"[81] Though she had journeyed far from her island homeland to start a new life in America, she did not forget the people or land of her birth in her moment of triumph.

Jay-Z had been right when he dubbed "Umbrella" a winner. "I knew ['Umbrella'] was going to be a No. 1 record," he says. "I believe what happened with this album is that she found her voice. . . . It shows such growth for her as an artist. If you listen to the lyrics to that song, you know the depth and how far she's come."[82] She had come a long way. Only one question remained: Where would she go from here?

Chapter 6

In the Spotlight

With her Grammy, Rihanna had received the highest honor in the music world. She did not plan to stop there, however. She told one interviewer, "Success for me isn't a destination, it's a journey. Everybody is working to get to the top, but where is the top? It's all about working harder and getting better and moving up and up."[83] She planned to do just that.

Rihanna's string of musical successes, along with six-figure endorsement deals, made her one of the richest teens in the country. *People* magazine interviewed her—along with *Harry Potter* star Daniel Radcliffe, golfer Michelle Wie, and actress-singer Hilary Duff—for its July 23, 2007, issue. The article, which was titled "Young and Rich," questioned how the wealthiest teens in the world handled money. Rihanna admitted that, although she saves some of her earnings, she also likes to shop. She is careful with money, though, and prefers to buy things that will last or that she will use often. She did confess, however, that she splurges on makeup and shoes, especially her favorite brand, Christian Louboutin. She may drop a lot of money on accessories, but Rihanna does not only spend money on herself or on frivolous purchases. She also puts some of her fortune to work for charity.

An Unbalanced Schedule

Rihanna's income grew as she marketed her records. She also promoted products such as the Miss Bisou clothing line, LG

Chocolate phones, Clinique perfume, and Chevrolet vehicles. Although she claimed to have inherited her mother's workaholic tendencies, she worked such long hours that her producers worried about her health. According to Margeaux Watson of *Entertainment Weekly*:

> Fearing that Rihanna might burn out from the pressures and her grueling schedule, Jay-Z urged her to return to Barbados for a vacation. . . . She followed his advice, but after soaking

In addition to singing and recording, Rihanna kept herself busy promoting products such as the Miss Bisou clothing line for J.C. Penney. Here she poses with the Miss Bisou designer Michele Bohbot during the launch of the clothing line in 2006.

The Bajan Reaction to Rihanna's Win

When Rihanna won a Grammy, most Bajans were overjoyed that she was putting Barbados on the map. Rihanna often uses a trident—the three-pronged fishing spear on the Barbados flag—on her music covers and in her appearances.

Some islanders, however, criticized Rihanna's dress, her outspokenness to the press, and her attitude. A few said she snubbed them. Evan Rogers, her producer, responded by reminding people that Rihanna was still a teenager and that she was trying to promote the island.

On February 22, 2008, a few weeks after her Grammy win, Minister of Culture Steve Blackett read the following proclamation:

> Whereas the Government and the people of Barbados truly acknowledge and celebrate the remarkable achievements of Robyn Rihanna Fenty; And whereas such an accomplishment has brought significant honour and deserving recognition not only to Rihanna but also to her beloved country and has elevated Barbados to the forefront of the entertainment world . . . the Government of Barbados designates Robyn Rihanna Fenty an honorary Youth and Cultural Ambassador of this country.

Afterward, Rihanna thanked the people of her homeland for their support and told them how proud she was to be a Bajan.

Caribbean Hot 30, "Rihanna Named Cultural Ambassador," February 25, 2008. www.caribbeanhot30.com/index.php?categoryid=8&p2_articleid=7.

up some rays at the beach and enjoying a few home-cooked meals, she found herself itching to get back into the studio. "That has a lot to do with my youth," she says. "Younger people are usually very restless and can't keep quiet. But I am also very passionate about what I do."[84]

Her tightly packed schedule left little time for relaxation or fun. Dividing her time between her career and personal life was difficult because work took the majority of her hours each day. She estimated that she devoted 99 percent of her time to her career. Even leisure pastimes of listening to music or shopping often connected to her career in some way. In the midst of recording her music, advertising products, and posing for magazine photo shoots, Rihanna also went on tour to attract international attention for her latest album.

Tour Headliner

Following the release of her earlier albums, she had opened for other singers while on tour. Now she was the star of her own

Rihanna was overwhelmed by fan turnout to her concerts in Europe, as these fans demonstrate in Mainz, Germany, in 2007.

Good Girl Gone Bad tour. The six-month tour, with its forty scheduled shows, took her to Canada, Europe, and the United States from September 2007 through April 2008. She shared billing with Akon in Canada. In the United Kingdom, Ciara, Caramel Luv, and David Jordan joined her in concert. She also held a free concert in Sofia, Bulgaria. Everywhere she went, excited fans greeted her.

While talking to a reporter following a concert in Serbia, Rihanna admitted that she was bewildered by the turnout. The expected crowd of six thousand people turned into a throng of twenty-four thousand on the night of the concert. Although she had three best-selling albums and songs that had reached number one, she still could not believe that so many people had come to see her. She was stunned that fans were screaming for her, because she still viewed herself as an ordinary girl.

Though she had trouble picturing herself as a star, others did not. In fact, some of the people in Belgrade thought she was spoiled. They complained because Rihanna's people requested the use of a Mercedes and a variety of special foods and snacks for her. In addition, the concert started almost two hours late because the security fence around the stage had cracked from the press of the crowds. Rihanna did not go on until the problem had been fixed, then she cut the concert shorter than anticipated. This led some people to conclude that she was a diva.

Time Out

U.K. audiences wondered, too, if she were getting arrogant when she canceled three shows in a row in December 2007. Her manager told reporters that she needed to rest her voice. Rather than talking, she had to write notes to people for several days. Even after she returned to her regularly scheduled tour dates, some audience members were annoyed when she was late for concerts. Others said she was performing robotically and not exerting real effort. They wondered if stardom had made her conceited or if overwork had exhausted her. Rihanna later told a reporter, "I just got so sick as I've been going for so long and haven't paced myself properly. My body just gave up and the

Chris Brown

C hristopher Maurice Brown, born May 5, 1989, grew up in Tappahannock, Virginia. Discovered at age thirteen, Brown went on to work with Jive Records and, by age sixteen, had a number-one single on the U.S. *Billboard* chart. He credits his father with helping him break into the industry. While working at a gas station, Brown's father met a producer and suggested he listen to his son.

Even after Brown had a recording contract and went on tour, his parents still insisted he do his homework. He left school in 2004 and was homeschooled so he could record his albums. His first album, *Chris Brown*, went platinum and generated three top-ten singles. The song "Run It!" was included on the album and debuted at number one. His second album, *Exclusive*, included the number-one hit "Kiss Kiss."

Brown is also a songwriter (he started at age fourteen), an actor, a dancer, and a music-video director. He has appeared with many other stars, including Rihanna and Jordin Sparks.

Although the press has often linked his name with Rihanna's, Brown insists they are just good friends. Regarding photos of them looking romantic, he once said, "I think we've got the worst luck with pictures." When asked how he could stop the rumors, Brown quipped, "Be yourself and see as many girls as possible!"

Quoted in Shawn Adler and Tim Kash, "Rihanna, Chris Brown Say It Again: They're 'Just Friends'—Although 'We've Got the Worst Luck with Pictures,'" MTV, March 31, 2008. www.mtv.com/news/articles/1584491/20080331/rihanna.jhtml.

doctors ordered me to rest. It was very upsetting letting people down but I feel much better now."[85]

In spite of that, as soon as Rihanna felt better she returned to her frantic pace. Def Jam's decision not to release a complete new album in the summer of 2008 allowed her time to recover from her exhaustion and vocal strain. During that time Rihanna recorded three new songs. They hit the market as singles, but they were also added to her previous album, which was then rereleased as *Good Girl Gone Bad: Reloaded*. The album came out in June 2008, just as her original album marked its historic fifty-second week on the *Billboard* 200 chart.

Chart Hopping

The first of the three singles to be released, "Take a Bow," was written by Ne-Yo. In the video a haughty Rihanna informs her boyfriend that she sees through his act. He tries to attract her attention as she drives away, but she ignores him. Later, she burns his clothing on the table. As often happens, the tabloids wondered if the song were based on Rihanna's relationship with Chris Brown. Some suggested that the male actor in the video resembled him. Once again, Rihanna reiterated that she and Brown were only friends.

"Take a Bow" debuted at number fifty-three in May 2008, then jumped fifty-two spots to number one on the *Billboard* Hot 100—the second-largest leap to number one in *Billboard* history. The only song to make a greater jump was Maroon 5's "Makes Me Wonder," which the year before had moved up from number sixty-four. "Take a Bow" became Rihanna's third number-one single. It was her first song to reach number one on the Black Entertainment Television *106 & Park: BET's Top 10 Live* video countdown. "Take a Bow" also had high digital sales: It sold 267,000 copies in the first week.

Another Collaboration

Rihanna made no secret of the fact that she admired Chris Brown, Maroon 5, and Kanye West or that she hoped to work with these artists someday. Her opportunity to team up with each of them came much sooner than she had expected. When she recorded her next releases, she collaborated with two of the three singers on her list.

Her second single, following "Take a Bow," was a remix of a Maroon 5 song written by group members Adam Levine and James Valentine. They had recorded the original for their second album, *It Won't Be Soon Before Long*. Although the song was almost complete, Levine wanted to add to it, so he invited Rihanna to join them in the studio. He said he chose Rihanna for her beauty and her talent. Maroon 5 believed she would be the best choice for what they had in mind.

When the group approached her, Rihanna was overjoyed. She had always wanted to work with Maroon 5 because it was one of her favorite groups. She felt honored that the band members asked her to record with them. The performers worked well

Rihanna with Adam Levine of the band Maroon 5 in 2008.

together, and both Rihanna and Maroon 5 added the song "If I Never See Your Face Again" to their upcoming albums. Levine was surprised to find that everything came together so quickly, but he believes that "if the magic is there, if the chemistry is there, you don't even have to think about it."[86]

The same magnetism was there for both of them. Rihanna and Maroon 5 discovered that the chemistry between them was strong. Levine acknowledged that he often has trouble concentrating when he is in the studio. Having Rihanna there made it even more difficult. Rihanna admitted that she, too, felt the attraction. When a reporter from *People* magazine asked her to describe Levine, she called him "hot." The magic continued as they teamed up for the video.

"I don't do a lot of videos where I have so much chemistry with the other artist; this is only my second duet in a video," Rihanna said at the time. "It's really intense, because you have to work with each other so much. It's new for me, but I'm enjoying it."[87] For Levine, the video was a departure from his usual style. Before he worked with Rihanna on this project, he rarely did any preplanning; instead, he preferred impromptu performances. This time, though, the choreography was scripted, and he found he liked the new method.

Best Friends

If Rihanna felt a spark with Levine, it was nothing compared to the one between her and Chris Brown, at least according to the press. Brown and his team, Graffiti Artizts, had written a song, "Disturbia." Originally, they planned to record it for the rerelease of Brown's album *Exclusive*, but Brown decided a female should sing it instead. He offered it to Rihanna. Def Jam wanted to save the song for her 2009 album, but Rihanna recorded it as another summer release. "Disturbia" was a bit different than most of her songs. The music retained the upbeat, rhythmic, dance tempo of many of her earlier releases, but the dark and depressing lyrics exuded the pain of mental anguish.

Interestingly enough, when "Disturbia" came out in June 2008, it debuted higher than any of her previous singles. It

Despite rumors that they are romantically involved, Rihanna insists that she is just very good friends with singer Chris Brown. The two of them attended the BET Awards together in 2008.

started at number eighteen on the *Billboard* Hot 100, then moved up to number eleven. "Disturbia" put Rihanna in a class with Janet Jackson and Shania Twain: All three were the only female artists to have six or more Top 40 Hot 100 hits from the same album.

The "Disturbia" collaboration brought something new into Rihanna's life, if the media reports were correct. They claimed the two singers had more than a working relationship. As in the past, if Rihanna appeared with a male in public even once, speculation began about a romantic connection between them. Chris Brown and Rihanna spent quite a bit of time together. Paparazzi followed the couple around and snapped pictures of them at restaurants, out shopping, or at parties.

Should Charity Begin at Home?

Some people question why with all Rihanna's money and generosity to various charities, her father, Ronald Fenty, sells toys, perfume, and household items from the trunk of his car. He makes about £250 ($500) a week, whereas Rihanna makes millions each year. He claims he does not want money from her: "The only thing I want is to be a part of her life. I have had her forgiveness, which you can't put a price on, and I would never dream of asking her for a dollar." He continues:

> She kissed me goodbye [after a concert] and I didn't notice her slipping something into my pocket. But when I got to the airport, I pulled out a wad of notes. It brought tears to my eyes. I would never ask her for money, but of course it came in handy. She rings me all the time and tells me she loves me. That's reward enough for me.

Nick Owens, "Rihanna Caught Her Dad Smoking Crack," *Sunday Mirror*, February 17, 2008. www.mirror.co.uk/sunday-mirror/2008/02/17/rihanna-caught-her-dad-smoking-crack-98487-20321828/.

When asked about their relationship, Rihanna claimed that he was one of her closest friends because they had a lot in common. They had both started their careers at about the same time. Both of them had been discovered as young teens and had become almost instant successes in the music world. They enjoyed spending time together, but Rihanna and Brown insisted that their relationship was more like brother and sister. Part of their connection, in addition to their close friendship, is their music. Soon after they met, Rihanna indicated that she hoped to sing a duet with Brown at some point. She made it clear that this desire did not mean she was in love with him; instead, it resulted from her love of music.

Fulfilling Dreams

Rihanna had an opportunity to collaborate with Brown during the Glow in the Dark Tour, which ran from April through August 2008. At some shows Brown performed his remix of "Umbrella," called "Cinderella," with Rihanna. Singing with him allowed her to fulfill one of her dreams. On the Glow in the Dark Tour, she also spent time with Kanye West. He had organized the tour and invited Rihanna to join him, Lupe Fiasco, and N.E.R.D.

Concerts were scheduled mainly in North America, although two months of shows were held in Europe. Singers Common and Estelle opened for the tour in the United Kingdom. The American singers developed close relationships as they traveled. By the time the tour was over, they had become like family, so it was hard for them to go their separate ways.

Wrapping up the tour allowed Rihanna to spend more time on other projects. She recorded songs for other performers' albums—for example, "Tears Fall" for Ciara's *Fantasy Ride* album and a remake of "The Tide Is High" for Kardinal Offishalls' album *I Am Not 4 Sale*. She fulfilled another dream—becoming an actress—with a role in *Mama Black Widow*. She also attended fashion shows in Europe that gave her ideas for her own clothing line.

Rihanna had one additional dream that she confided to a reporter from *People* magazine:

> When I was young and I would watch television and I would see all the children suffering, I always said when I grow up I want to help. Not long after, I was in the position where I could help. I started to visit all these children's hospitals and I have a soft spot for kids. I just want to help and make sure they are happy.[88]

Helping Others

To help children, Rihanna started her own charity in 2006, the Believe Foundation. She conducts fund-raisers and offers concerts for children. The money she collects provides medical assistance and helps needy youngsters. In 2008 she partnered with Def Jam and Escada Moon Sparkle fragrance to sponsor a tour called "A Girl's Night Out." After the concerts she held meet-and-greet sessions for terminally ill children, during which she signed autographs and had pictures taken with them. In addition to the Believe Foundation, Rihanna has also performed at benefits for the United Nations Children's Fund (UNICEF). One of her ad campaigns for Gucci, called "Tattoo Heart," also provided money for UNICEF.

Children are not the only ones who have benefited from Rihanna's generosity. Lisa Gershowitz Flynn, the mother of two young children, discovered she had leukemia and needed a bone

Rihanna set up the Believe Foundation to help children. Here she talks with a young fan at a Believe Foundation charity event in 2008.

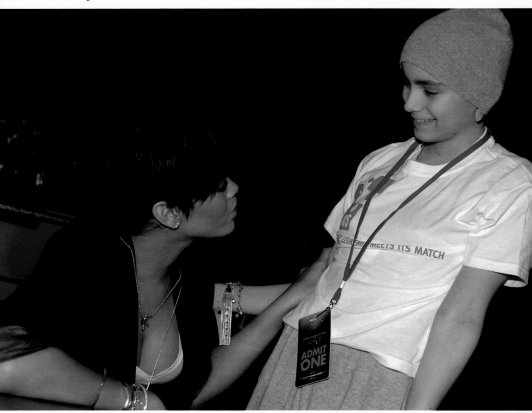

Rihanna and Charity

Founded by Rihanna in 2006, the Believe Foundation is a charity that supports children in need around the world. According to its mission statement:

> Believe gives children a chance to not only survive, but thrive in a world where many will never receive the medical attention, school supplies, toys and clothes that they deserve. The foundation is committed to creating change in the lives of our youth by providing educational, financial, social and medical support when and wherever it is needed. Rihanna and the Believe Foundation are committed to helping our children succeed by granting them the tools they need to believe.

After she helped leukemia patient Lisa Gershowitz Flynn, a mother with two children, Rihanna extended her support to the Deutsche Knochenmarkspenderdatei donor center to help it find bone marrow donors. By saving adults, her charity is also helping children, who need their parents.

Some of the other charities Rihanna has supported include Designers Against AIDS, Live Earth (which combats the global climate crisis), Mission Australia (which provides housing for the homeless and jobs for the unemployed), Raising Malawi (which helps orphans in this poor African country), and the Red Cross.

Believe Foundation, 2006. www.believerihanna.com.

marrow transplant to live. Determined to help Flynn, Rihanna contacted the press and began a campaign to find a bone marrow donor for her. More than five thousand people offered to donate bone marrow to Deutsche Knochenmarkspenderdatei, one of the largest donor centers in the world. Two thousand of these volunteers became new donors.

Flynn was overwhelmed. She was amazed that a star as well known as Rihanna would take the time to help others when her own career was so demanding. She publicly expressed her gratitude for the donor match and for the singer's willingness to aid her family. Rihanna responded, "I feel honored to be a part of such an amazing miracle. This blessing has continued to keep me aware of how precious life really is. I will be praying for Lisa and her family as they move into a hopeful future."[89]

Future Possibilities

From the time she was young, Rihanna focused on the future. Hers definitely looks bright. With more album deals in the works, she can continue to make her childhood dream of singing all around the world a reality. "I was born to do it. I eat, sleep, drink, cry, and laugh music. I love music, I have a passion for it and it comforts me."[90]

She has had many chances to pursue her aspirations. Along with reaching her own goals, she hopes to inspire others. Rihanna realizes that as a celebrity she can have an impact on many people's lives. She hopes to be a positive influence on those around her. "I always wanted to make a difference in the world. I was always trying to figure out how can I change the world."[91] One way she accomplishes this is by being a role model for the many children who look up to her. As she told one young fan who asked her how to succeed, "Never give up on your dreams! Keep working, stay positive!!!"[92] Rihanna's story provides a shining example of how hard work and determination can make dreams come true.

Introduction: Barbados Cinderella

1. Quoted in Chris Rolls, "Exclusive Interview with Rihanna," MP3.com, May 15, 2006. www.mp3.com/news/stories/4525.html&print=1.

Chapter 1: Her Island Home

2. Quoted in 7 Confessions, "Rihanna on the Cover of *You* Magazine," December 10, 2007. http://7confessions.blogspot.com/2007/12/rihanna-on-cover-of-you-magazine.html.

3. Quoted in *Entertainment News*, "Doctors Thought Rihanna Had Brain Tumour," June 23, 2007. www.pr-inside.com/entertainment-blog/2007/06/23/doctors-thought-rihanna-had-brain-tumour/.

4. Quoted in Maureen Paton, "The Dark Secret in Raunchy Pop Sensation Rihanna's Past," *You*, November 2007. www.mailonsunday.co.uk/you/article-492706/The-dark-secret-raunchy-pop-sensation-Rihannas-past.html.

5. Quoted in Nick Owens, "Rihanna Caught Her Dad Smoking Crack," *Sunday Mirror*, February 17, 2008. www.sundaymirror.co.uk/news/sunday/2008/02/17/rihanna-caught-her-dad-smoking-crack-98487-20321828/.

6. Quoted in Suzannah Ramsdale, "Rihanna's Dad Apologises for Being a Crack Addict," *Now*, September 4, 2007. www.nowmagazine.co.uk/celebrity-news/242177/rihanna-s-dad-apologises-for-being-a-crack-addict/1/.

7. Ramsdale, "Rihanna's Dad Apologises for Being a Crack Addict."

8. Quoted in Margeaux Watson, "Caribbean Queen: Rihanna," *Entertainment Weekly*, June 29, 2007. www.ew.com/ew/article/0,,20043393,00.html.

9. Quoted in Watson, "Caribbean Queen."

10. Quoted in Bang Showbiz, "Rihanna's Brother War," AskMen.com, June 7, 2007. www.askmen.com/gossip/rihanna/rihannas-brother-war.html.

11. Quoted in Owens, "Rihanna Caught Her Dad Smoking Crack."

12. Quoted in Tom Bryant, "Rihanna: I Grew Up with a Crack Addict Dad," *Sunday Mirror*, December 18, 2007. www.mirror.co.uk/news/topstories/2007/12/18/rihanna-i-grew-up-with-crack-addict-dad-89520-20259307/.

13. Quoted in Paton, "The Dark Secret in Raunchy Pop Sensation Rihanna's Past."
14. Owens, "Rihanna Caught Her Dad Smoking Crack."
15. Owens, "Rihanna Caught Her Dad Smoking Crack."
16. Quoted in Sylvia Patterson, "Singing in the Rain," *Observer*, August 26, 2007. http://music.guardian.co.uk/pop/story/0,,2153943,00.html.
17. Quoted in Patterson, "Singing in the Rain."

Chapter 2: A Bold Move

18. Quoted in Watson, "Caribbean Queen."
19. Quoted in MSN Entertainment, "Rihanna," October 25, 2007. http://msninconcert.msn.com/music/Rihanna/en-id/article.aspx.
20. Quoted in Jennifer Bisram, "Rihanna on the Rise: The Barbados-born Beauty Gets Her Big Break!" MoraFire.com, March/April 2008. www.morafire.com/index.php?option=com_content&task=view&id=29&itemid=36.
21. Quoted in Patterson, "Singing in the Rain."
22. Quoted in Beverly Smith, "The Good, the Bad, the Rihanna," *PaperMag*, July 13, 2007. www.papermag.com/?section=article&parid=2055&page=1.
23. Quoted in Bisram, "Rihanna on the Rise."
24. Jason Birchmeier, "Rihanna: *Music of the Sun*."
25. Quoted in Rolls, "Exclusive Interview with Rihanna."
26. Quoted in ARTIST direct, "Exclusive Interview with Rihanna!" May 12, 2006. www.artistdirect.com/nad/news/article/0,,3655378,00.html.

Chapter 3: Topping the Charts

27. Justin Lewis, "Rihanna's *Music of the Sun*: If It's Good Music That You Want, Make Rihanna Your Girl!" *Associated Content,* September 27, 2006. www.associatedcontent.com/article/63895/rihannas_music_of_the_sun_if_its_good.html.
28. Quoted in Bisram, "Rihanna on the Rise."
29. Quoted in "Rihanna: Brightest Star," AllHipHop.com, September 19, 2005. http://allhiphop.com/stories/alternatives/archive/2005/09/19/18135471.aspx.
30. Birchmeier, "Rihanna."
31. Tasha Matiu, "Rihanna: Official Rihanna." Bebo.com. http://upload.bebo.com/Profile.jsp?MemberId=3203033271.
32. Quote in *People*, "Rihanna Biography: Rihanna's Debut," August 30, 2005. www.people.com/people/rihanna/biography.

33. Bruce Britt, "Rihanna," *BMI Music World*, February 22, 2006, www.bmi.com/musicworld/entry/533081.

34. Quoted in Rihanna Site, "Rihanna Quotes," 2007. www.rihannasite.info/rihanna-quotes.html.

35. Quoted in Starpulse.com, "Rihanna's *A Girl Like Me* Out Now," April 26, 2006. www.starpulse.comews/index.php/2006/04/26/rihanna_s_a_girl_like_me_out_now_listen_.

36. Quoted in Rihanna Site, "Rihanna Quotes."

37. Lewis, "Rihanna's *Music of the Sun*."

38. Quoted in Rolls, "Exclusive Interview with Rihanna."

39. Quoted in Starpulse.com, "Rihanna's *A Girl Like Me* Out Now."

40. Quoted in Duane Booth, "Flashback: Rihanna," Aboutmag.com, August 2006. http://aboutmag.com/main/?p=214.

41. Quoted in Rolls, "Exclusive Interview with Rihanna."

42. Quoted in Basil Walters, "Rihanna for Smile Jamaica-Africa Unite," *Melodymakers.de*, January 18, 2008, www.melodymakers.de/forum/showthread.php?t=7171.

43. Quoted in ARTIST direct, "Exclusive Interview with Rihanna!"

44. Quoted in Booth, "Flashback."

45. KOvideo.net, "Rihanna: *Unfaithful* Song Review." www.kovideo.net/music/video/Rihanna---Unfaithful/35.html.

46. Quoted in ARTIST direct, "Exclusive Interview with Rihanna!"

47. Rolls, "Exclusive Interview with Rihanna."

Chapter 4: Lonely at the Top

48. Quoted in Sindy, "Rihanna Interview," Kidzworld, 2005. www.kidzworld.com/article/5853-rihanna-interview.

49. Quoted in Superiorpics.com, "Rihanna." www.superiorpics.com/rihanna/.

50. Quoted in Bang Showbiz, "Rihanna's Bull Detector," AskMen.com, May 26, 2008. www.askmen.com/gossip/rihanna/rihannas-bull-detector.html.

51. Quoted in Dan Cairns, "Rihanna's Growing Pains," *Nation News*, December 28, 2007. www.nationnews.com/story/330030140590964.php.

52. Quoted in Cairns, "Rihanna's Growing Pains."

53. Quoted in Paton, "The Dark Secret in Raunchy Pop Sensation Rihanna's Past."

54. Quoted in Beverley Lyons and Laura Sutherland, "Umbrella Star Rihanna Sick of Fake Pals," *Daily Record*, May 27 2008. www.dailyrecord.co.uk/entertainment/entertainment-news/2008/05/27/umbrella-star-rihanna-sick-of-fake-pals-86908-20430701/.

55. Quoted in AskMen.com, "Interview: Rihanna," July 2007. www.ask men.com/toys/interview_200/206_rihanna_interview.html.

56. Quoted in Bryant, "Rihanna."

57. Quoted in *World Entertainment News*, "Rihanna Tired of 'Bubbly' Showbiz Persona," May 6, 2008. www.pr-inside.com/entertainment-blog/2008/ 05/06/rihanna-tired-of-bubbly-showbiz-persona/.

58. Paton, "The Dark Secret in Raunchy Pop Sensation Rihanna's Past."

59. Quoted in Contact Music.com, "Rihanna—Rihanna Refuses to Pose Nude," August 10, 2008. www.contactmusic.com/new/xmlfeed.nsf/mndwebpages/rihanna%20perfects%20her%20autograph.

60. Quoted in *Cosmopolitan*, "Rihanna Reigns," *Cosmopolitan*, March 2008. www.cosmopolitan.com/celebrities/exclusive/Rihanna-Reigns.

61. Quoted in Lyons and Sutherland, "*Umbrella* Star Rihanna Sick of Fake Pals."

62. Quoted in Jayson Rodriguez, "Rihanna's 'Painful' *Umbrella* Shoot Kept Her on Her Toes: VMA Lens Recap," MTV.com, September 5, 2007. www.mtv.com/news/articles/1568860/20070904/rihanna.jhtml.

63. Quoted in Rodriguez, "Rihanna's 'Painful' *Umbrella* Shoot Kept Her on Her Toes."

64. Quoted in Rodriguez, "Rihanna's 'Painful' *Umbrella* Shoot Kept Her on Her Toes."

65. Quoted in Contact Music.com, "Rihanna."

66. Paton, "The Dark Secret in Raunchy Pop Sensation Rihanna's Past."

67. Quoted in Watson, "Caribbean Queen."

68. Quoted in 7 Confessions, "Rihanna on the Cover of *You* Magazine."

Chapter 5: Awards Rain Down

69. Quoted in Rihanna Site, "Rihanna Quotes."

70. *InStyle*, "Transformation: Rihanna," 2008. www.instyle.com/instyle/celebrities/transformation/0,,20210008,00.html?cid=recirc-people Recirc.

71. Quoted in Bryant, "Rihanna."

72. Quoted in Nekesa Mumbi Moody, "Rihanna Releasing New Single, 'Umbrella,'" Yahoo! Music, March 29, 2007. http://music.yahoo.com/read/news/41857031.

73. Quoted in BelgradeNet.com Travel Guide, "Rihanna in Belgrade," November 2007. www.belgradenet.com/announcements.html.

74. Talia Kraines, "Music—Artists and Albums: Rihanna: *Good Girl Gone Bad*," BBC, June 14, 2007. www.bbc.co.uk/music/release/32bd/.

75. Jason Kennedy, "Rihanna: *Good Girl Gone Bad* Reviews," *Portrait*, 2007. www.portraitmagazine.net/reviews/albums/goodgirlgonebad. html.

76. Quoted in Watson, "Caribbean Queen."

77. Quoted in Watson, "Caribbean Queen."

78. AllHipHop.com, "Rihanna: *Good Girl Gone Bad*," June 8, 2007. http://209.18.98.81/reviews/index.asp?ID=1217.

79. Kraines, "Music."

80. Quoted in Cairns, "Rihanna's Growing Pains."

81. Maria Bradshaw, "Grammy Girl," *Nation News*, February 11, 2008. www.nationnews.com/story/290977982429101.php.

82. Quoted in *People*, "Celebrity Central: Rihanna," 2008. www.people. com/people/rihanna.

Chapter 6: In the Spotlight

83. Quoted in Rihanna Fenty.com, "Rihanna Quotes." http://rihanna-fenty.com/html/rihanna/quotes.html.

84. Watson, "Caribbean Queen."

85. Quoted in Bryant, "Rihanna."

86. Quoted in James Montgomery and Yasmine Richard, "Rihanna, Maroon 5 Team Up for 'Magic' Collaboration, Complete with Ultra-glam Video," *MTV*, April 24, 2008. www.mtv.com/news/articles/1586264/20080424/rihanna.jhtml.

87. Quoted in Montgomery and Richard, "Rihanna, Maroon 5 Team Up for 'Magic' Collaboration, Complete with Ultra-glam Video."

88. Quoted in Stephen M. Silverman, "Rihanna Touring for Kids in Need," *People*, March 27, 2008. www.people.com/people/article/0,,20186594,00.html.

89. Quoted in K.C. Baker, "Rihanna 'Honored' to Be Part of Leukemia Miracle," *People*, March 13, 2008. www.people.com/people/article/0,,20183928,00.html.

90. Quoted in Bisram, "Rihanna on the Rise."

91. Quoted in Patterson, "Singing in the Rain."

92. Quoted in Patterson, "Singing in the Rain."

1988

Robyn Rihanna Fenty is born on the Caribbean island of Barbados on February 20.

2003

Rihanna sings for music producer Evan Rogers, who invites her to New York to record a demo tape.

2004

Def Jam signs Rihanna for a six-album deal.

2005

Rihanna releases her first album, *Music of the Sun*, and tours with Gwen Stefani.

2006

The Believe Foundation, Rihanna's charity to help children in need around the world, opens.

January 2006

Barbados honors Rihanna at the Barbados Music Awards with eight awards.

April 2006

A Girl Like Me, Rihanna's sophomore album, comes out less than a year after her first album.

October–December 2006

To promote *A Girl Like Me*, Rihanna joins Jay-Z and Ne-Yo on the Rock Tha Block Tour in Australia and tours with the Pussycat Dolls.

2007

Rihanna records "Umbrella" with Jay-Z, and the single later skyrockets from number forty-one to number one.

May 2007

Good Girl Gone Bad, Rihanna's third album, marks a change in her style and attitude.

September 2007

Rihanna begins her tour to promote her album *Good Girl Gone Bad*; the tour continues until April 2008.

2008

"Umbrella" captures a Grammy Award for Best Rap/Sung Collection.

April 2008

"Take a Bow," a single written with Ne-Yo, leaps from number fifty-three to number one on the *Billboard* Hot 100.

June 2008

Rihanna's fourth album, titled *Good Girl Gone Bad: Reloaded*, comes out and includes new singles "Disturbia" by Chris Brown and "Rehab" with Justin Timberlake.

Books

Dennis Abrams, *Jay-Z*. New York: Chelsea House, 2007. An exploration of Jay-Z's rise from the streets of New York to the head of a recording company.

James Hooper, *Chris Brown*. Broomall, PA: Mason Crest, 2007. The story of Chris Brown's remarkable breakthrough into the music scene as a young teen and his subsequent career accomplishments.

Heidi Krumenauer, *Rihanna*. Hockessin, DE: Mitchell Lane, 2008. A short biography of Rihanna's life from her discovery to her third album release.

Internet Sources

Cosmopolitan, "Rihanna Reigns," March 2008. www.cosmopolitan.com/celebrities/exclusive/Rihanna-Reigns. Information on Rihanna's persona change, love life, and career are covered by this article.

Dorian Lynskey, "Sweetness and Steel," *Guardian*, May 23, 2008. www.guardian.co.uk/music/2008/may/23/urban. A newspaper article about Rihanna on the set of the video shoot for "If I Never See Your Face Again." Reveals details of her past, her busy lifestyle, and the Bajan reaction to her fame.

Monsters & Critics, "Rihanna—Musicians," 2008. www.monstersandcritics.com/people/archive/peoplearchive.php/Robyn_Rihanna_Fenty_. A database of articles, photos, and biographical information about Rihanna.

People, "Celebrity Central: Rihanna," 2008. www.people.com/people/rihanna. The latest news on Rihanna from *People* magazine includes a timeline of all of her major accomplishments, her biography, recent photos, breaking news, and an archive of previous articles.

SuperiorPics.com, "Rihanna," 2008. www.superiorpics.com/rihanna/. A series of photos from Rihanna's major public appearances, with a short biography and facts about Rihanna's life.

Linda Wells, "Rihanna Lets Down Her Guard," *Allure*, January 2008. www.allure.com/magazine/2008/01/rihanna. This article offers candid shots and information about Rihanna's life and interests. The Web site contains a behind-the-scenes look at Rihanna prepping for her cover shoot.

Web Sites

Official Rihanna Web Sites

Believe Foundation (www.believerihanna.com). This is the official Web site for Rihanna's charity.

Def Jam (www.defjam.com). Type in Rihanna's name for information on her latest releases, tours, and awards.

MySpace: Rihanna (www.myspace.com/rihanna). Rihanna's MySpace page provides photos, music and ringtone downloads, a blog, and a message board.

Rihanna (www.rihannanow.com). This is Rihanna's official Web site, with news, tour dates, information, and her products for sale.

Fanzines

Rihanna (http://rihannasite.com/). This site bills itself as the biggest Rihanna fan site around. It has a frequently updated blog with information on Rihanna's appearances, endorsements, music, and videos.

Robyn Rihanna Fenty (www.robynrihannafenty.com/). This tribute to Rihanna contains news and updates, photos, biographical information, quotes, and message boards. It has a Barbados emphasis and flavor.

Ultimate Rihanna (http://www.ultimate-rihanna.com). This site contains news, a photo gallery, message boards, and answers to fans' questions.

Additional Web Resources

Contactmusic (www.contactmusic.com). Enter Rihanna's name at this site for audio and video clips, stories, pictures, and music reviews.

Entertainment Weekly (www.ew.com). Find news and current articles about Rihanna by typing in her name at this site.

ETonline (www.etonline.com). A search for Rihanna's name brings up photos and news stories at this Web site.

Internet Movie Database (www.imdb.com). Search for Rihanna to find a list of her soundtracks and movie credits as well as news articles and a brief biography.

Last.FM (www.last.fm). At this site, type in Rihanna's name to play videos, download music, and access information on up-coming events.

People (www.people.com). At *People* magazine's Web site, search for Rihanna to find the latest celebrity news and photos of her and her friends.

TV.com (www.tv.com). Learn about Rihanna's television appearances by searching under her name on this site. It also includes a brief biography.

About the Author

Laurie J. Edwards is a multi-published author and editor of books for both children and adults under several pseudonyms. A former librarian and teacher, she enjoys researching and writing about a variety of topics. Edwards has more than 750 magazine articles and educational pieces in print. She and her husband have five children and divide their time between North Carolina and Pennsylvania.